HATCHMENTS IN BRITAIN

8

Cheshire, Derbyshire, Leicestershire, Lincolnshire, Nottinghamshire and Staffordshire

8

Cheshire, Derbyshire, Leicestershire, Lincolnshire, Nottinghamshire and Staffordshire

Edited by

PETER SUMMERS, F.S.A.
and
JOHN E. TITTERTON

PHILLIMORE

1988

Published by
PHILLIMORE & CO. LTD.
Shopwyke Hall, Chichester, Sussex

ISBN 0 85033 652 X

*Thanks are due to the Manifold Trust,
whose support enabled this book to be published*

Printed and bound in Great Britain by
OXFORD UNIVERSITY PRESS

CONTENTS

ILLUSTRATIONS

GENERAL INTRODUCTION

Hatchments are a familiar sight to all those who visit our parish churches. They are not only decorative, but of great interest to the herald, genealogist and local historian. It is therefore surprising that — apart from local surveys in a few counties mostly in recent years — no attempt has yet been made to record them on a national scale. This series will, it is hoped, remedy the deficiency; it is proposed to publish separate volumes covering all English counties as well as Wales, Scotland and Ireland.

It is probable that no volume will be complete. Previously unrecorded hatchments will turn up from time to time; many have already been found in obscure places such as locked cupboards and ringing chambers. There are likely to be some inaccuracies, for hatchments are often hung high up in dark corners, and the colours may have faded or be darkened with age and grime. Identification is a problem if the arms do not appear anywhere in print: and even if the arms are identified, pedigrees of the family may not always be available. But enough has been done to make publication worth while; the margin to the pages will perhaps allow for pencilled amendments and notes.

Since I began the survey in 1952 many hatchments, probably evicted at the time of Victorian restorations, have been replaced in the churches when they came. On the other hand, during the same period just as many hatchments have been destroyed. An excuse often made by incumbents is that they are too far gone to repair, or that the cost of restoration is too great. Neither reason is valid. If any incumbent, or anyone who has the responsibility for the care of hatchments which need attention, will write to me, I shall be happy to tell him how the hatchments may be simply and satisfactorily restored at a minimal cost. It is hoped that the publication of this survey will help to draw attention to the importance of these heraldic records.

The diamond-shaped hatchment, which originated in the Low Countries, is a debased form of the medieval achievement — the shield, helm, and other accoutrements carried at the funeral of a noble or knight. In this country it was customary for the hatchment to be hung outside the house during the period of mourning, and thereafter be placed in the church. This practice, begun in the early 17th century, is by no means entirely obsolete, for about 80 examples have so far been recorded for the present century.

Closely allied to the diamond hatchment, and contemporary with the earlier examples, are rectangular wooden panels bearing coats of arms. As some of these bear no inscriptions and a black/white or white/black background, and as some otherwise typical hatchments bear anything from initials and a date to a long inscription beginning 'Near here lies buried...', it will be appreciated that it is not always easy to draw a firm line between the true hatchment and the memorial panel. Any transitional types will therefore also be listed, but armorial boards which are clearly intended as simple memorials will receive only a brief note.

With hatchments the background is of unique significance, making it possible to tell at a glance whether it is for a bachelor or spinster, husband or wife, widower or widow. These different forms all appear on the plate immediately following this introduction.

Royal Arms can easily be mistaken for hatchments, especially in the West Country where they are frequently of diamond shape and with a black background. But such examples often bear a date, which proves that they were not intended as hatchments. Royal hatchments, however, do exist, and any examples known will be included.

All hatchments are in the parish church unless otherwise stated, but by no means are they all in churches; many are in secular buildings and these, if they have no links with the parish in which they are now found, are listed at the end of the text. All hatchments recorded since the survey began are listed, including those which are now missing.

As with the previous volumes much work has been done in the past by many friends; their records have proved invaluable and greatly lessened the amount of research needed. As for those now responsible for each county who have checked and added to all these early records, I am most grateful for their care and efficiency. For the last two volumes I was greatly helped by John Titterton as Assistant Editor. For the remainder of the series he is Co-Editor.

The Illustrations on the following two pages are the work of the late Mr. G. A. Harrison and will provide a valuable 'key' for those unfamiliar with the complexity of hatchment backgrounds.

One last, but important note. Every copy sold of this book helps a child in the Third World; for I have irrevocably assigned all royalties on the entire series to a charity, The Ockenden Venture.

PETER SUMMERS
Paddocks, Reading Road, Wallingford

1. MARRIED MAN
2. MARRIED WOMAN
3. BACHELOR
4. WIDOW
5. WIDOWER
6. SPINSTER

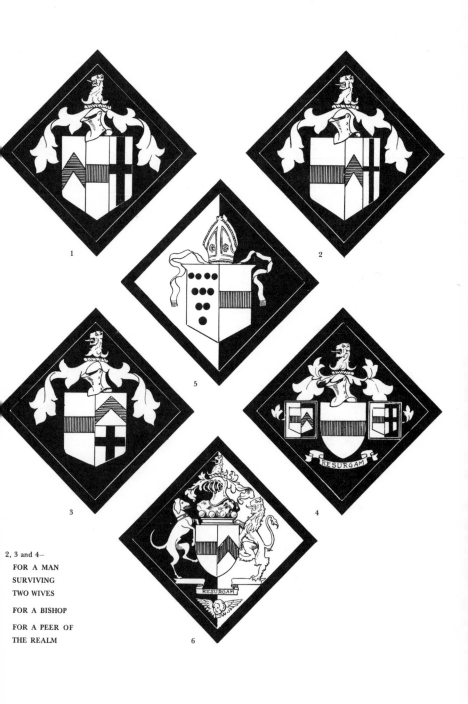

1

2

5

3

4

6

2, 3 and 4—
  FOR A MAN
  SURVIVING
  TWO WIVES

  FOR A BISHOP

  FOR A PEER OF
  THE REALM

ABBREVIATIONS

B.P.	= Burke's *Peerage, Baronetage and Knightage*
B.L.G.	= Burke's *Landed Gentry*
B.E.P.	= Burke's *Extinct and Dormant Peerages*
B.E.B.	= Burke's *Extinct and Dormant Baronetcies*
V.C.H.	= *Victoria County History*
D.N.B.	= *Dictionary of National Biography*
M.I.	= Monumental Inscription
P.R.	= Parish Register
M.O.	= *Musgrave's Obituary*
G.M.	= *Gentleman's Magazine*
Gen. Mag.	= *Genealogists' Magazine*
M.G. & H.	= *Miscellanea Genealogica et Heraldica*
Ormerod	= *The History of the County Palatinate and the City of Chester*
Earwaker	= *East Cheshire, Past and Present*
T.H.S.L.C.	= *Transactions of the Historical Society of Lancashire and Cheshire*
Venn	= *Alumni Cantabrigiensis*
Nichols	= *The History and Antiquities of the County of Leicester*
Lincs Peds	= *Lincolnshire Pedigrees*, Harleian Society, Vols. L to LV

NOTE

Blazons throughout are exactly as noted at the time of recording, not as they ought to be.

CHESHIRE

by

James Blundell

Bowdon: for George, 1st Earl of Warrington, 1819
(*Photograph by Mr. D. G. Richbell*)

INTRODUCTION

A meagre tally of 63 surviving hatchments in the county would appear to lend poor support to Cheshire's proud boast of having been 'the seed-plot of the gentry' but losses have clearly been substantial. Some indication of their extent is afforded by the fact that from one church alone, Astbury St Mary, no less than a score of hatchments disappeared at the time of Sir Gilbert Scott's restoration in 1862. Losses continue to occur though, happily, not on such an extensive scale with the present situation and condition of a number of hatchments giving cause for concern regarding their prospects of survival. On the credit side of the balance sheet, however, the rescue of the Armitstead hatchment from probable destruction suggests the possibility that there might be others in private hands which have escaped notice. Also the restored Brooke hatchment at Church Minshull serves as an exemplar for those churchwardens and incumbents who are becoming increasingly aware that, notwithstanding its historical interest, a century and a half old hatchment in poor condition is likely to detract from, rather than enhance, the architectural merit of its surroundings.

Whilst the hatchments recorded in the ensuing inventory cover a period of two and a half centuries from 1717 to 1968 all but nine are for individuals who died in the 19th century. Those commemorated comprise a random collection of peers, baronets, clerics, members of parliament, country squires and the odd banker, envoy and manufacturer together with their ladies. Husbands and wives or widows are, indeed, represented by separate hatchments in no fewer than nine instances. Three alone of our subjects, Cotton and the clerics Raikes and Wrangham, were deemed to merit articles in the *Dictionary of National Biography* and of this trio only Field Marshal Sir Stapleton Cotton, Viscount Combermere, can be accounted a figure of national renown. It was his generalship which secured victory for the British troops at Salamanca and Talavera and

3

earned for him the augmentations to his arms and crest which are features of his hatchment at Wrenbury.

The connoisseur of esoteric forms of marshalling will find that the Jacson hatchment at Bebington illustrates an unusual, but by no means unique, method of combining the arms of husband and two wives and that of Nathaniel Maxey Pattison at Congleton affords a late instance of the not uncommon Tudor practice of dimidiating an impaled quarterly coat of arms.

Misplaced quarters and errors of tincture are quite common and ignorance of the function of the lozenge is revealed at Malpas where the arms of Mrs. Thomas Crewe Dod are depicted on 'this singularly inconvenient form of shield' despite the fact, suggested by the parti-coloured background, that she was survived by her husband. Further solecisms were committed at Congleton and Lawton where crests are to be seen incorporated in the hatchments of Mrs. Pattison and Mrs. Lawson respectively and at Cholmondeley and Malpas where the two hatchments of the 1st Marquess of Cholmondeley depict his lordship's arms encircled by the Garter and the collar of a G.C.H. with those of his lady in pretence. Insignia of knighthood or of office are also to be seen associated with the arms of Viscount Combermere, Sir Arthur Aston, and the 5th Marquess of Cholmondeley, and Sir Richard Puleston's hatchment incorporates the crest he was granted in 1806 to commemorate his having introduced the Prince of Wales into his Principality.

The most interesting group of hatchments in the county is undoubtedly that in the Cholmondeley chapel where a series of six commemorates the present marquess's five predecessors in the title together with the first marquess's widow. The first and second marquess are also commemorated by hatchments in Malpas church and in the parish church at Houghton where the family's Norfolk estates are located. The purists might, with some justification, argue that the 'hatchments' of the 4th and 5th marquesses, painted 40 years and five years respectively after their subjects' deaths, appear in the inventory under false colours since they clearly never fulfilled their primary function. There is, however, good reason to believe that the former is, in fact, a replica of an original which could have served to advertise its subject's death.

The so-called Randle Holme's memorial tablets which are a feature of a number of Cheshire churches and total, indeed, more than the surviving hatchments were considered to be outside the scope of this survey. A detailed inventory of those at Stoak, Thornton-le-Moors and Backford was published in vol. xxi (1905) of the *Transactions of the Lancashire and Cheshire Historic Society.*

James Blundell,
100, Mossley, Congleton

ADLINGTON Hall
1. All black background
On a lozenge   Qly of six, 1st, Sable a chevron between three bulls'
heads cabossed argent (Wright), 2nd, Argent on a fess gules three
roundels (   ), 3rd, Argent a fleur-de-lys within an orle and eight
martlets sable (Wynington), 4th, Azure on a fess between three stags
trippant or a trefoil azure (Robinson), 5th, Per chevron sable and argent
(Aston), 6th, Argent on a bend azure three mascles argent (Adderley),
impaling, Per chevron paly of six vert and or counterchanged, in chief
two squirrels respectant proper (Adnutt)
Motto: Sublimiora quaero
For Mary Catherine, dau. of the Rev. Thomas Adnutt, Rector of Croft,
who m. the Rev. Henry Wright, of Mottram Hall, and d. 29 Dec.
1867.   (B.L.G. 5th ed.)

ASTON
1. All black background
On a circular shield within the Order of the Bath   Per chevron
argent and sable (Aston)
Crest: An ass's head erased per pale argent and sable   Mantling:
Gules and argent   Motto: Resurgam   Supporters: Dexter, A
griffin qly argent and gules, beaked and pendant from a collar or an
escutcheon, Argent on a fess gules three escallops or   Sinister, An
ounce sable collared as dexter with an escutcheon, Gules on a bend
argent three trefoils slipped azure   Skull in base
For Sir Arthur Ingram Aston, G.C.B., of Aston, Envoy Extraordinary
and Minister Plenipotentiary at the Spanish Court from 1839 to 1843, d.
unm. 5 May 1859.   (Ormerod, i., 725; M.I.)

BEBINGTON, St Andrew
1. Dexter and centre background black
Qly, 1st and 4th, Or a fess between three sheldrakes proper (Jacson),
2nd, Gules a saltire between four annulets or (Shallcross), 3rd, Gules
three lions rampant or (Fitzherbert), impaling, two coats per pale, 1.
Azure three storks rising argent (Gibson), 2. Or a chevron between three
lions' heads erased or (Johnson)
Crest: A sheldrake proper   Mantling: Gules and argent   Motto:
Resurgam
For the Rev. Roger Jacson, A.M., who m. 1st, 1777, Frances, dau. of the
Rev. John Gibson, and 2nd, 1801, Mary Anne Johnson, and d. 6 Mar.
1826, aged 72.   (Alumni Cantabrigienses, M.I.)

7

2. All black background
Gules a fess dancetty argent (Orred), impaling, Qly, 1st and 4th, Argent
a fess and a canton gules (Woodville), 2nd and 3rd, Argent a fess
voided, on a canton gules a cross moline or (   )   To dexter of
main shield, Argent a cross engrailed gules, over all a bend azure (for
Tranmere)   To sinister of main shield, Sable three stags' heads
cabossed argent (Bebington)
Crest: A hare courant proper   Mantling: Gules and
argent   Motto: illegible
For George Orred, who m. 1803, Frances, dau. of William Woodville, of
Edge Hill, Lancs, and d. 1 July 1825, aged 54.   (B.L.G. 1898 ed.;
Ormerod, ii, 437)

3. All black background
A circular shield with decorative border   Azure three stags trippant
or, on a chief or three crescents sable (Green)
Crest: A demi-stag per fess or and azure charged with two crescents in
pale counterchanged   Mantling: Gules and argent   Motto:
Resurgam   Skull below
For Joseph Green, who d. unm. 8 April 1829.   (B.L.G. 18th ed.;
Ormerod, ii, 43)

4. Dexter background black
Green, as 3., but stags or ermined sable, impaling, Paly of eight argent
and gules (Henley)
Crest: As 3.   Mantling: Very flowery, gilded   Motto: Resurgam
For Richard Green, who m. Jane Henley (d. 1852), and d. 8 April
1845.   (Sources, as 3.)

BOWDON
1. Dexter background black
Qly, 1st and 4th, Barry of six argent and azure (Grey), 2nd and 3rd,
Argent three boars' heads erect and erased sable (Booth), impaling,
Azure a cross moline argent (Bentinck)
Earl's coronet   Crest: On a chapeau gules and ermine a wyvern
passant or   Mantling: Gules and ermine   Mottoes: A ma
puissance, and below it, Resurgam   Supporters: Dexter, A unicorn
ermine armed and maned or   Sinister, A lion double-queued sable
For George, 5th Earl of Stamford and 1st Earl of Warrington, who m.
1763, Henrietta, dau. of William, 2nd Duke of Portland, and d. 28 May
1819.   (B.P. 1949 ed.)
(There are further hatchments attributed to the 5th Earl at Enville,
Staffs and Groby, Leics.)

BURTON
1. All black background
Sable a chevron between three battleaxes argent (Congreve), impaling,
Azure three fleurs-de-lys a canton argent (Birch)

Crest: A falcon rising proper belled or   Mantling: Gules and
argent   Mottoes: (above crest) Persevere   (below shield) Non
moritur cujus fama vivit   Cherubs' heads at top corners of shield
and winged skull below
For Richard Congreve, of Burton, who m. 1801, Mary Anne, dau. of
George Birch, of Hampstead Hall, Staffs, and d. Nov.
1857.   (B.L.G. 5th ed.; Ormerod, ii., 554 ff.)

CAPESTHORNE Hall
1. All black background
On a lozenge surmounted by a cherub's head   Argent three chaplets
vert flowered gules (?Faulder), impaling, two quarterly coats per pale:
1. Qly, 1st and 4th, Argent a chevron between three cross crosslets fitchy
sable (Davenport), 2nd and 3rd, Azure a cross formy argent (Ward); 2.
Qly, 1st, Davenport, 2nd, Argent a fess between three calves gules
(Calveley), 3rd, Argent a chief azure (Haselwall), 4th, Gules three bars
ermine a lion rampant or (Bagnal)
Motto: Resurgam
Unidentified

CHESTER, St John
1. All black background
Argent a chevron engrailed sable ermined or between three griffins'
heads erased sable each charged with an ermine spot or (Raikes),
impaling, Gules a fess paly of four or and azure in dexter chief an
annulet or for difference (Whittington)
Crest: A griffin's head erased sable charged with an ermine spot
or   Mantling: Gules and argent   Motto: Spes mea in
deo   Winged skull below
For the Rev. Canon Henry Raikes, Chancellor of the diocese of Chester,
who m,. 1809, Augusta, dau. and heiress of Jacob Whittington, of
Yoxford Lodge, Suffolk, and d. 28 Nov. 1854. She d. 24 Oct.
1820.   (B.L.G. 1937 ed.)

2. Dexter background black
Argent three garbs or, on a chief azure three bezants
(Wrangham)   In pretence: Sable two lions passant in pale paly of
six argent and gules, a canton argent (Strangways)
Crests: Dexter, A dove volant, in its beak an olive branch
proper   Sinister, A lion passant paly of six argent and
gules   Mantling: Gules and or   Motto: Hyeme
exsuperata   Winged skull below
For the Ven. Francis Wrangham, F.R.S., Prebendary of York and
Chester, who m. 2nd, Dorothy, dau. of the Rev. Digby Cayley, by
Elizabeth, dau. of Thomas Robinson (the family having in consequence
of the will of Luke Robinson, of Riseborough, laid aside their former

name of Strangways), and d. 27 Dec. 1842.   (Burke's Commoners,
II, 311; D.N.B.)

CHOLMONDELEY Castle

1. Dexter background black

Gules in chief two esquires' helms argent garnished or in base a garb or
(Cholmondeley)   In pretence: Argent three battering rams in pale
proper (Bertie)   All within the Garter, with the George pendant
below
Marquess's coronet   Crest: A demi-griffin sable, winged and beaked
or, holding between the claws a helm as in the arms   Mantle:
Gules and ermine   Motto: Cassis tutissima virtus   Supporters:
Dexter, A griffin sable, winged and beaked or   Sinister, A pilgrim or
friar vested russet with his exterior hand resting on a crutch and
suspended from his belt a rosary both or
For George James, 1st Marquess of Cholmondeley, K.G., who m. 1791,
Georgiana Charlotte, 2nd dau. of Peregrine, 3rd Duke of Ancaster, and
d. 10 April 1827.   (B.P. 1949 ed.)
(There are other hatchments for the 1st Marquess, at Malpas, and at
Houghton, Norfolk)

2. All black background

On a lozenge   Qly, 1st and 4th, Cholmondeley, 2nd, Gules a
chevron between three griffins' heads erased argent (   ), 3rd, Or on
a fess between two chevrons sable three cross crosslets or
(Walpole)   In pretence: Bertie
Marchioness's coronet   Supporters: Dexter, as 1.   Sinister, as 1.,
but vested grey, crutch proper and rosary argent
For Georgiana Charlotte, widow of George James, 1st Marquess of
Cholmondeley. She d. 23 June 1838.   (B.P. 1949 ed.)
(There is another hatchment for Lady Cholmondeley at Houghton,
Norfolk)

3. Dexter background black

Cholmondeley, impaling, Qly, 1st and 4th, France, 2nd and 3rd,
England, a bordure compony argent and azure (Somerset)
Marquess's coronet   Crest and motto: As 1.   Mantle: Gules and
argent   Supporters: Dexter, as 1.   Sinister, A wolf or collared
azure
For George Horatio, 2nd Marquess of Cholmondeley, who m. 2nd, 1830,
Susan, 4th dau. of Henry, 6th Duke of Beaufort, and d.s.p. 8 May
1870.   (B.P. 1949 ed.)
(There are other hatchments for the 2nd Marquess, at Malpas, and at
Houghton, Norfolk)

4. All black background

Gules in chief two esquires' helms argent in base a garb or
(Cholmondeley), impaling, Qly, 1st and 4th, Azure a crescent between
three molets argent (Arbuthnot), 2nd and 3rd, qly i. & iv. Argent a fess
between two chevrons azure (Lisle), ii. & iii. Azure on a chevron
between three herons argent three fleurs-de-lys sable (Clapcott)
Marquess's coronet   Crest: As 1., but helm ungarnished   Motto:
As 1.   Supporters: Dexter, A griffin sable, winged, beaked and
membered or, langued sable   Sinister, A wolf or collared
vair   All on a mantle gules and argent fringed and corded or
For William Henry Hugh, 3rd Marquess of Cholmondeley, who m.
1825, Marcia Emma Georgiana, dau. of the Rt. Hon. Charles Arbuthnot,
and d. 16 Dec. 1884.   (B.P. 1949 ed.)
(There is another hatchment for the 3rd Marquess at Houghton,
Norfolk)

5. All black background

Cholmondeley, as 4., impaling, Argent ten escallops four, three, two and
one sable, on a canton gules a molet pierced or (Kingscote)
Marquess's coronet   Crest: As 4.   Motto: As 1.   Mantling:
Gules and argent   Supporters: As 4.   Signed in base, N.M.
1963.
For George Henry, 4th Marquess of Cholmondeley, who m. 1879,
Winifred Ida, dau. of Col. Sir Robert Kingscote, and d. 16 Mar.
1923.   (B.P. 1949 ed.)
(This hatchment was painted by Norman Manwaring)

6. All black background

Cholmondeley arms only, as 1.
Marquess's coronet   Crest and motto: As 1.   Mantle: Gules and
argent   Supporters: As 4.   Behind the shield two staves in
saltire argent, and suspended from the base of the shield on a blue
ribbon a key fesswise ward downwards to dexter, the handle composed of
a royal crown surmounted by the monogram ER within a circlet all or
(Office of Lord Great Chamberlain)   Signed in base, N.M. 1973.
For George Horatio, 5th Marquess of Cholmondeley, Lord Great
Chamberlain, who m. 1913, Sybil, only dau. of Sir Albert Sassoon, Bt.,
and d. 16 Sept. 1968.   (B.P. 1949 ed.)
(This hatchment was painted by Norman Manwaring: there is another
hatchment for the 5th Marquess at Houghton, Norfolk)

CHURCH MINSHULL
1. Dexter background black

Or a cross engrailed qly gules and sable, in dexter chief a crescent gules
(Brooke), impaling, Sable three conies courant argent (Cunliffe)
Crest: A brock proper   No mantling   Motto: In coelo
quies   Winged skull in base   In a gilded wooden frame (recent)
For Thomas Brooke, of Church Minshull, 2nd son of Sir Richard

Brooke, 4th Bt., m. 1787, Margaret (d. 6 Dec. 1826), youngest dau. of Sir
Robert Cunliffe, Bt., and d. 20 June 1820, aged 65.   (Ormerod, i.,
677/8 and 685; B.P. 1949 ed.; Cheshire Sheaf, 3rd ser., xxxii, 89; Foster,
Alumni Oxon.; Annual Register 1820)

CONGLETON

1. Sinister background black

Qly, 1st and 4th, Azure on a chevron argent between three hearts or
three talbots' heads erased argent (for Pattison), 2nd and 3rd, Gules a
fess between three talbots' heads erased argent (for Maxey), impaling,
Ermine three bars azure on a canton gules a fleur-de-lys or
(Comberbach)
Crest: A talbot's head erased argent   Mantling: Gules and
argent   Motto: In coelo quies   Winged skull in base
For Helen, dau. of Roger Comberbach, protonotary of the county
palatine of Chester, who m. Nathaniel Maxey Pattison, of West House,
Congleton, and d. 6 Nov. 1818, aged 54.   (M.I. in church)

2. All black background

Two coats per fess, in chief, Pattison with escallops azure, and in base,
Maxey, both impaling, Barry of six ermine and azure on a canton gules
a fleur-de-lys or (Comberbach)
Crest: A talbot's head erased argent   Mantling: Gules and
argent   Motto: In coelo quies   Winged skull in base
For Nathaniel Maxey Pattison, who d. 13 Aug. 1827, aged
66.   (M.I.)

3. All white background

Azure a bend counter-embattled argent in chief a crescent argent
(Malbon)
Crest: A griffin's head erased proper   Mantling: Gules and argent
For William Malbon, of Dane Bank, Congleton, son of John Gorst,
maltster, assumed the name and arms of Malbon in 1791 in compliance
with the will of Samuel Malbon, and d. unm. 11 Dec. 1826, aged
70.   (Par. Regs. of Astbury and Congleton; Keeper of MSS, Edin.
Univ. Libr.; Cowdroy's Directory and Guide to Chester, 1789)

4. All black background

On a lozenge   Qly, 1st and 4th, Argent a chevron between three
cormorants sable (Warburton of Arley), 2nd and 3rd, Qly argent and
gules in second and third quarters a fret or (Dutton), impaling, Argent a
chevron embattled sable between three stags' heads cabossed proper
(Parker)
For Alice, dau. of the Rev. John Parker, of Astle, who m. Sir Peter
Warburton, 5th Bt., of Arley, and d. 9 Sept. 1837.   (M.I. in Gt
Budworth church)

DUNHAM MASSEY
1. Dexter background black
Qly, 1st and 4th, Barry of six argent and azure (Grey), 2nd and 3rd, Argent three boars' heads couped and erect sable langued gules (Booth) No helm or mantling   Earl's coronet   Crest: A unicorn ermine, armed, maned, tufted and unguled or in front of a sun in splendour proper   Supporters: Two unicorns ermine, armed, maned, tufted and unguled or   Motto: A ma puissance
For George Harry, 7th Earl of Stamford and 3rd Earl of Warrington, who d.s.p. 2 Jan. 1883.   (Ormerod, i., 534; B.P. 1949 ed.; Complete Peerage)

DUNHAM MASSEY Hall
1. Sinister background black
Qly, 1st and 4th, Barry of six argent and azure (Grey), 2nd and 3rd, Argent three boars' heads couped and erect sable (Booth), impaling, a diapered blank (for Billage)
Countess's coronet   Supporters: Two unicorns ermine, armed, maned and unguled or
For Elizabth, dau. of John Billage, of Wincanton, Somerset, who m. 1848, as his 1st wife, George Harry, 7th Earl of Stamford and 3rd Earl of Warrington, and d.s.p. 22 Oct. 1852.   (Complete Peerage)

EATON
1. All black background
Lozengy or and azure on a pale gules three estoiles or (Antrobus) Crest: Issuing from rays proper a unicorn's head couped argent, horned and maned or, gorged with a laurel wreath vert   No helm or mantling   Motto: Dei memor gratus amicis
For Gibbs Crawford Antrobus, of Eaton Hall, High Sheriff of Cheshire, 1834, d. 21 May 1861.   (Earwaker, ii., p. 650)

INCE
1. All black background
On a lozenge surmounted by three cherubs' heads
Qly, 1st and 4th, Gules a fess chequy argent and azure between three stags' heads cabossed argent and a bordure or (Park), 2nd and 3rd, Gules three falcons close belled or (Atherton), in centre chief a molet or for difference   In pretence: Argent a fess azure between three gates proper (Yates)
Motto: In coelo quies   Winged skull in base
For Elizabeth Jane, dau. and heiress of Edmund Yates, of Ince Hall, who m. the Rev. William Waldegrave Park (son of Sir James Allan Park, and Lucy, dau. of Richard Atherton), vicar of Kirk-Whelpington, and d. 17 July 1856.   (M.I.; D.N.B.; Foster, Alum. Oxon.)

KNUTSFORD
1. All black background
Qly, 1st and 4th, Azure two bars or over all a bend gules (Legh), 2nd,
Azure a chevron or ermined sable between three arrows palewise points
downwards or, on a chief or three daws sable beaked and membered
gules, on a canton gules a molet or (Dawson), 3rd, Or five fusils
conjoined in fess azure (Bold)
Crest: An arm erect couped at the shoulder sleeved gules cuffed argent
holding a sword erect argent entwined by a serpent all
proper   Mantling: Gules and argent   Motto: Resurgam
For Peter Legh, of Booths, who d. unm. 29 Aug. 1857, aged
63.   (Ormerod, i., 320, 500, iii., 893; THSLC vol. 7, p. 72, Chetham
Soc. Pubs. 88, 231)

LAWTON
1. Sinister background black
Argent on a fess between three cross crosslets fitchy azure a cinquefoil
argent (Lawton), impaling, Qly, 1st and 4th, Argent a fess of three fusils
gules a bordure azure (Montagu), 2nd and 3rd, Or an eagle displayed
sable (Monthermer), a crescent or on fess point of impalement
Crest: A demi-wolf rampant reguardant argent   Mantling: Gules
and argent   In base a tomb chest with cherub's head at either
end   On wood panel, and of fusil rather than lozenge shape
For Anne, dau. of George, younger son of Henry, 1st Earl of Manchester,
who m. as his 1st wife, John Lawton of Lawton, and d. 1 July 1717. He
d. 10 June 1736.   (B.L.G. 7th ed.; Ormerod iii., p. 11)

2. Dexter background black
Argent on a fess between three cross crosslets fitchy sable a cinquefoil
argent (Lawton), impaling, Qly, 1st and 4th, Azure a lion rampant
argent (Crewe), 2nd, Gules fretty and semy-de-lys or (Hamelyn), 3rd,
Argent on a cross flory azure a lion passant or (Offley)
Crest and mantling: As 1.
For John Lawton of Lawton, who m. Anne (d. 29 Nov. 1810), younger
dau. and co-heir of Charles Crewe, M.P., and d. 25 Mar.
1804.   (M.I.; B.P. 1937 ed.)

3. All black background
Lawton, as 2.
Crest and mantling: As 1.   Date under shield, 1831
For William Lawton of Lawton, who d. unm. 9 Mar. 1831.   (B.L.G.
1937 ed.; Cheshire Record Office)

4. Dexter background black
Lawton, as 2., impaling, Azure two bars argent a bend compony or and
gules (Legh of Adlington)
Crest and mantling: As 1.

For John Lawton of Lawton, who m. 1843, Emily Anne, dau. of Thomas
Crosse Legh of Adlington, and d. 9 June 1864.   (M.I.; B.L.G. 1937
ed.)

5. Dexter background black
Lawton, as 2., impaling, Azure three garbs or (Erskine)
Crest: As 1.   Mantling: Sable and argent   Motto: Resurgam
For William John Percy Lawton of Lawton, who m. Mary Maud, dau.
of the Hon. Edward Erskine, and d. 8 Nov. 1883.   (B.L.G. 1937 ed.)

6. Dexter background black
Lawton, as 2., impaling, Gules three fleurs-de-lys argent (   )
Crest and mantling: As 1.   Motto: Spes infracta
Unidentified

LYMM
1. Dexter background black
Qly, 1st and 4th, Gules an eagle displayed ermine armed or, a chief
chequy or and azure (Halstead), 2nd, Azure a lion rampant argent
collared gules (Domville), 3rd, Gules a pale fusilly argent (Lymm),
impaling, Gules two lions' gambs erased chevronwise between three
hawks' lures or (Chesshyre)
Crest: A griffin's head erased ermine   No mantling   Motto:
Nulla pallescere culpa   Shield surrounded with an ornamental cord
For the Rev. Domville Halstead, LL.B., of Dane Bank, Lymm, who m.
Elizabeth, dau. of John Chesshyre, of Warrington, and was buried at
Lymm, 31 Dec. 1781.   (Ormerod, i., 577 ff.; Venn, Pt. I, ii., 292)

2. All black background
On an asymmetric lozenge surmounted by a winged cloud
Arms: As 1.
Mantling (from cloud): Gules and argent
For Elizabeth, widow of the Rev. Domville Halstead, buried at Lymm, 3
Jan. 1795.   (Sources, as 1.)

3. All black background
Qly, 1st and 4th, Azure a lion rampant within an orle of fleurs-de-lys
argent (Poole), 2nd, Halstead, 3rd, Domville   In pretence: Gules
three fleurs-de-lys or (Massey of Rostherne)
No helm   Crest: A griffin's head per fess or and azure issuing from a
ducal coronet or   Mantling: Gules and argent   Motto: As 1.
For Domville Poole, of Dane Bank, son and heir of the Rev. Domville
Halstead, who m. Sarah, dau. and co-heiress of James Massie, of
Manchester and Rostherne, and d. at Bath, 26 Apr.
1795.   (Ormerod, i., 557 ff.; Venn, II, v., 154; Alum. Oxon.;
Manchester School Register, vol. 1)

4. All black background
Qly, 1st and 4th, Sable a lion passant argent (Taylor), 2nd, Domville,
3rd, Qly gules and or in the first quarter a lion passant or (Massey of
Lymm)   In pretence: Argent two bars gules (Mainwaring)
Crest: A talbot passant argent   Mantling: Gules and
argent   Motto: Coelestia post haec   Skull in base
For Massie Taylor of Lymm, who m. Anne, dau. of George Mainwaring,
of Bromborough, and d.s.p. 1 Jan. 1769.   (Ormerod, i., 577 ff.;
Venn, I, iv., 207; C.R.O. DDX 367/1 & 2)

5. All black background
Qly, 1st, Taylor, 2nd, Massey of Lymm, 3rd, Domville, 4th,
Lymm   In pretence: Gules a cross patonce or (Jackson)
Crest: A tiger statant proper   Mantling: Gules and
argent   Motto: Mors janua vitae   Cherub's head at each top
angle of shield, and winged skull in base
For Thomas Taylor of Lymm, who m. Mary, dau. of Samuel Jackson, of
Ash, co. Salop, and d. 27 Jan. 1814.   (Sources, as 4.)

6. All black background
Qly, 1st, Sable a lion passant argent collared gules (Taylor), 2nd,
Massey of Lymm, 3rd, Azure a lion rampant argent (Domville), 4th,
Lymm
Crest: A talbot passant argent   Mantling: Gules and
argent   Motto: In coelo quies   Cherub's head at each top angle
of shield and winged skull in base
Probably for Massie Taylor, of Moss Hall, Audlem, and Abbots
Grange, Chester, younger brother of Thomas Taylor (No. 5), d. unm. 29
June 1821, aged 69.   (Sources, as 4.; Ormerod, iii., 472; Cheshire
Sheaf, 3rd series, xi (1914), p. 43 and xliii (1948), pp. 47-49)

7. Dexter background black
Qly, 1st, Taylor, as 4., 2nd, Massey of Lymm, 3rd, Domville, as 6., 4th,
Lymm   In pretence: Qly, 1st and 4th, Or a chevron between three
boars' heads couped close sable (   ), 2nd and 3rd, Or a lion
rampant gules (   )
Crest, mantling and motto: As 6.   Winged skull in base
Probably for Robert Taylor of Lymm, eldest son and heir of Thomas
Taylor (No. 5), who m. Jane, dau. of the Rev. John Foulkes, of Mostyn,
and was buried at Lymm, 20 Feb. 1835.   (Sources, as for 5.;
Manchester School Register, vol. ii., p. 76)

MACCLESFIELD
1. All black background
Qly, 1st, Argent a chevron sable between three brocks statant proper, in
centre chief a molet gules for difference (Brocklehurst), 2nd, Or a lion
rampant sable langued gules and charged on the shoulder with a cross

formy argent (Pownall), 3rd, Gules three garbs or (   ), 4th, as 1st,
but no molet   In pretence: Qly, 1st and 4th, Sable a chevron ermine
between three lions' heads erased or (Unett), 2nd, Azure on a chevron
between three escallops argent three leopards' faces gules (   ), 3rd,
Ermine a cross patonce sable (   )
Crests: Dexter, A brock statant proper   Sinister, Out of a ducal
coronet or a demi-lion sable   No helm or mantling   Motto:
Veritas me dirigit   Inscribed around frame: Thomas Brocklehurst
AD 1823 married Martha Mary Unett. They died AD 1870 Thomas
aged 79, Martha Mary aged 72 years. Their children shall arise and call
them blessed.
For Thomas Brocklehurst, son of John Brocklehurst by his second wife,
dau. and heiress of Peter Pownall, m. 1823, Martha Mary, dau. of
Thomas Unett, of Market Drayton, and d. 7 Nov. 1870, aged
79.   (B.P. 1970 ed.; B.L.G. 18th ed.; Earwaker, 11, 420 et seq.)

MALPAS
1. Identical to Cholmondeley Castle, No. 1., q.v.

2. Identical to Cholmondeley Castle, No. 3, q.v., except that the
sinister supporter is not collared, and the mantle is gules and ermine

3. All black background
Qly, 1st, Gules a chevron or ermined sable between three cinquefoils or,
in chief a crescent or for difference (Tarleton), 2nd, Gules six fleurs-de-
lys, three, two and one or (Ireland), 3rd, Ermine a bend engrailed azure
(English), 4th, as 1st, but no crescent   In pretence: Qly, 1st, Vert a
chevron between three stags trippant or (Robinson), 2nd, Per chevron
embattled argent and sable three gates counterchanged (Yates), 3rd,
Argent a chevron between three martlets gules (   ), 4th, Argent on a
bend azure a   in chief or (   )
Crest: On a mural crown gules between two ostrich feathers argent a
tiger's head proper   Mantling: Gules and argent   Motto: Post
nubila phoebus   Cherub's head at each top corner of shield and
winged skull in base
For Thomas Tarleton, of Bolesworth Castle, who m. Mary, 3rd dau. and
co-heiress of Lawrence Robinson, of Clitheroe, Lancs, and d. 2 Jan.
1820.   (Ormerod, ii., p. 677)

4. Sinister background black
Qly, 1st and 4th, Tarleton, with quatrefoils and both with the crescent
in chief or, 2nd, Gules six fleurs-de-lys, three, one and two or (Ireland),
3rd, Argent a bend engrailed azure (English)   In pretence: Qly, 1st,
Robinson, 2nd, Yates, 3rd, as 3., 4th, Gules on a bend engrailed argent
a   in chief sable (   )
No helm, crest, mantling or motto   Cherub's head resting on head
of shield

For Mary, 3rd dau. of co-heiress of Lawrence Robinson, and wife of
Thomas Tarleton (No. 3), d. at Bath 12 Feb. 1812, and bur. at
Malpas.   (Source, as 3.)

5. Sinister background black
On a lozenge surmounted by three cherubs' heads
Argent on a fess gules cotised wavy sable three crescents or (Dod),
impaling, Argent a scythe and in fess point a fleur-de-lys sable (Sneyd)
Motto: Mors janua vitae   Skull in base
For Anne, 4th dau. of Ralph Sneyd of Keele, co. Staffs, who m. Thomas
Crewe Dod of Edge, and d. 25 Nov. 1826.   (Ormerod, ii., 682)
(This hatchment is very unusual in that the arms are borne on a lozenge
instead of a shield)

6. All black background
Arms: As 5.
Crest: A serpent vert issuing from and piercing a garb or   Mantling:
Gules and argent   Motto: In copia cautus   Cherub's head at
each top angle of shield and skull below
For Thomas Crewe Dod, of Edge, who d. 18 May 1827.   (Source, as
5.)

MOTTRAM, Hall Farm
1. Sinister background black
Qly, 1st and 4th, On a chevron embattled counterembattled sable
between three pheons azure two flaunches gules each charged with a
tilting spear or headed argent (Armitstead), 2nd and 3rd, Ermine a cross
voided between four fleurs-de-lys sable (Fenton), impaling, Qly gules
and or in the first and fourth quarters three fleurs-de-lys argent (Massie
of Doddington)
Mantling: Gules and or   Motto: Resurgam   Cherub's head
above shield
For Harriet Vyse, dau. of the Rev. Richard Massie of Coddington,
Rector of Aldford and St Bridget's, Chester, who m. 1829, Lawrence
Armitstead, of Cranage Hall, son and heir of the Rev. John Armitstead
of Middlewich, by his first wife, Katherine, dau. and co-heir of John
Fenton, of Betley and Newcastle-under-Lyme, and d. 17 July 1836. He
d. 31 Oct. 1874.   (Ormerod, iii., 123 & 131; B.L.G. 18th ed.; M.I.s
at Goostrey and Holmes Chapel)
(The property of Judge and Mrs. P. Curtis)

SHOCKLACH
1. Dexter background black
Qly of 12, 1st, Sable three molets argent (Puleston), 2nd, Chequy argent
and sable (Warren), 3rd, Argent two lions passant guardant azure
armed gules (Hanmer), 4th, Azure, three boars' heads passant argent
langued gules (   ), 5th, Sable three bulls' heads cabossed argent

langued gules (Bulkeley), 6th, Paly of six or and gules (   ), 7th, as
3rd, with a label of three points gules (Hanmer), 8th, Vert a lion
rampant or langued and armed gules (   ), 9th, Paly of six argent
and sable three bars gules (   ), 10th, Barry of six or and azure a
bend gules (   ), 11th, Argent three lions passant sable langued and
armed gules (   ), 12th, Argent a chevron sable between three ermine
tails (   ), in fess point of shield the Badge of Ulster
Crests: Dexter, On a mount vert an oak tree proper, pendant therefrom
an escutcheon gules charged with the Badge of the Prince of
Wales   Sinister, On a chapeau gules and ermine a buck statant
proper   Mantlng: Gules and argent   Motto: Clariores e tenebris
To dexter of main shield, Puleston, impaling, Azure a chevron ermine
between in chief two bucks salient argent langued gules and in base a
lion passant argent langued and armed gules (Boats) S.B1.   To
sinister of main shield, Puleston with Badge of Ulster, impaling, Or two
ravens in pale proper (Corbet)
For Sir Richard Puleston, 1st Bt., son of Richard Parry Price, by his
wife, Anne, sister of John Puleston of Emral, m. 1st, Ellen, dau. of John
Boats, of Liverpool, and 2nd, Emma Elizabeth, dau. of John Corbet, of
Sundorne Castle, co. Salop, and d. 19 May 1840.   (B.P. 1894 ed.;
M.I.s in Worthenbury church)
(There is an identical hatchment for Sir Richard in Worthenbury church,
Flintshire)

STOAK
1. Dexter background black
Argent on a bend sable three chessrooks argent, in chief the Badge of
Ulster (Bunbury), impaling, Argent two lions passant guardant azure
armed and langued gules (Hanmer)
Crest: Two swords in saltire proper pommels or through the mouth of a
leopard's face or   Mantling: Gules and argent   Motto: Firmum
in vita nihil
For Sir Henry Bunbury, 3rd Bt., who m. Susanna, dau. of William
Hanmer, of Bettisfield, co. Flint, and d. 12 Feb. 1732/33.   (B.P.
1949 ed.; M.I.)

2. All black background
On a lozenge surrounded by decorative scrollwork
Arms: As 1.
Motto: Memoria pii aeterna
For Susanna, widow of Sir Henry Bunbury, 3rd, Bt., d. 23 Sept.
1744.   (Sources, as 1.)

STOCKPORT
1. Dexter background black
Qly, 1st and 4th, Sable on a chevron between three bulls' heads
cabossed argent a crescent between two cross crosslets gules, in centre

chief a cross crosslet or for difference (Wright), 2nd and 3rd, Or a cross
parted and fretted gules between in the first and fourth quarters three
martlets and in the second and third quarters three annulets sable
(Street)   In pretence, Wright, but without difference mark
Crests: Dexter, Out of a ducal coronet or a bull's head cabossed
argent   Sinister, A demi-man in armour proper his breastplate
charged with a cross as in the arms and supporting with his dexter hand
a flagstaff from which flows to the dexter a banner gules charged with an
annulet or
Motto: Sublimiora quaero
For Capt. James Frederick D'Arley Wright, who m. 1857, Julia
Catherine, dau. and co-heiress of the Rev. Henry Wright of Mottram
Hall.   Capt. Wright (formerly Street) assumed the surname of
Wright by Royal Licence in 1865, and d. 15 Dec. 1889.   (B.L.G.
1894 ed.: Earwaker, ii., 354)

SWETTENHAM
1. All black background
On a lozenge surmounted by a cherub's head
Argent a fess sable between three lions rampant gules (Heys), impaling,
Gules two bars gemel between three escallops argent (Rigge)
For Anne, dau. of Roger Rigge, who m. John Heys, M.D., and d.
(Burke's Commoners i., 305)

TATTON PARK
1. Sinister background black
Argent a lion rampant gules between three pheons sable (Egerton),
impaling, Argent a chevron sable between three fountains (Sykes)
No helm, crest or motto   Three cherubs' heads above shield
For Elizabeth, 2nd dau. of Sir Christopher Sykes, Bt., of Sledmere, who
m. 1806, Wilbraham Egerton, of Tatton Park, and d. 28 Feb.
1853.   (B.P.; Ormerod, i., 446)

2. All black background
Arms: As 1.
Crest: A lion rampant gules supporting an arrow in pale point
downwards argent   Mantling: Gules and or   Motto: Sic donec
For Wilbraham Egerton, who d. 25 Apr. 1856.   (Sources, as 1.)

THORNTON-LE-MOORS
1. Dexter background black
Qly, 1st and 4th, Gules a bend argent (Folliott), 2nd and 3rd, Or a
chevron between three bucks' heads cabossed sable (Harwood)
Crest: A lion rampant per pale argent and gules   Mantling: Gules
and argent   Motto: Sic transit gloria mundi   Winged skull
below

Probably for William Harwood Folliott, who m. Catherine, dau. and
heiress of John Burscoe of Nantwich, and d. 22 Nov. 1831, aged 70. She
d. 30 May 1850, aged 78.   (M.I.)

2. Dexter background black
Argent on a chevron sable between three pinecones reversed proper three
leopards' faces argent (Perryn)   In pretence: Argent a saltire gules
(for Gerrard)
No helm   Crest: A pinecone erect or   Motto: Non omnis moriar
For the Rev. Richard Perryn, Rector of Standish, who m. Dorothy (d. 23
June 1826), dau. and heiress of George Edward Gerrard, of Trafford
Hall, and d. 31 Oct. 1825, aged 71.   (M.I.)

3. All black background
Perryn arms only
Crest: A pineapple erect or leaved and sprouting vert   Mantle:
Gules and argent   Motto: Spectemur agendo   Cherubs' heads at
top corners of shield and winged skull below
Probably for Richard Gerrard Perryn, of Trafford Hall, who m. Harriet
Barbara (d. 22 Feb. 1845, aged 44), dau. of Alexander Hatfield, and d. 8
July 1850, aged 59.   (M.I.)

4. Dexter background black
Qly, 1st and 4th, Perryn, 2nd and 3rd, Gerrard, impaling, Barry of ten
or and azure over all a bend gules (for Wallis)
Two helms and crests: Dexter, A pineapple erect or   Sinister, A
lion's gamb erased and erect sable, holding a hawk's lure or and
surmounted by the motto JEHOVAH JIREH in gold letters on blue
scroll (for Gerrard)   Mantling: Gules and argent fimbriated
or   Motto: Spectemur agendo
For the Rev. Gerrard Alexander Perryn, who m. 1857, Elizabeth
Massey, dau. of Sir Provo William Parry Wallis, and d. 19 Jan. 1878,
aged 54.   (M.I.)

5. All black background
On a lozenge surrounded by ornamental scrollwork
Arms: As 4.
Motto: Spectemur agendo
For Elizabeth, widow of the Rev. Gerrard Alexander Perryn, d. 2 Jan.
1890, aged 71.   (M.I.)

WEAVERHAM
1. Dexter background black
Qly, 1st and 4th, Argent three bendlets wavy azure (Wilbraham), 2nd
and 3rd, Azure two bars argent, on a canton azure a wolf's head erased
argent (Wilbraham), impaling, Azure a bend engrailed argent cotised or
(Fortescue)

Crest: A wolf's head erased argent   Mantling: Gules and
argent   Motto: Mors janua vitae   Winged skull in base
For George Wilbraham, of Delamere Lodge and Nantwich, who m.
1814, Anne, 3rd dau. of Hugh, 1st Earl Fortescue, and d. 24 Jan.
1852.   (B.L.G. 1898 ed.; M.I. in church; Ormerod, ii., 138)

WRENBURY
1. Dexter background black
Two roundels of arms   Dexter, within a circlet of the Order of the
Bath enclosed by two branches of laurel proper issuing from a scroll in
base bearing the words Ich Dien and encircled by the collar of the
Order of the Bath with its pendant badge flanked on dexter and sinister
respectively by the badges of a Knight Grand Cross of the Royal
Hanoverian Guelphic Order and of a Knight Grand Cross of the
Portuguese Order of the Tower and Sword, Qly, 1st and 4th, Sable a
chevron between three cotton hanks argent and in chief a cross formy or
suspended by a ribbon gules fimbriated azure (Cotton, with
Augmentation), 2nd and 3rd, Argent a lion rampant sable (Stapleton),
in fess point the Badge of Ulster   Sinister, within a decorative
circlet, arms as dexter with in pretence, Sable a bend between three
fleurs-dy-lys argent (Gibbings)
Viscount's coronet   Crests: Dexter, A falcon wings expanded proper
belled or holding in the dexter claw a belt azure buckled
or   Centre, On a mount vert a soldier of the 3rd Regt. of Light
Dragoons mounted all proper in the act of charging, and on a scroll
azure above the word SALAMANCA in gold letters (Crest of
Augmentation)   Sinister, Out of a ducal coronet or a Saracen's head
couped at the shoulders affronté wreathed at the temples argent and
sable   Motto: In utraque fortuna paratus   Supporters: On either
side a falcon wings expanded proper murally collared gules and belled
or holding a spear proper from which flies a pennon   All on a
mantle gules and argent
For Field-Marshal Sir Stapleton Cotton, Bt., cr. Viscount Combermere,
1827, G.C.B., K.S.I., K.T.S., G.C.H., P.C., who m. 1838, as his 3rd
wife, Mary Woolley, only dau. and heiress of Robert Gibbings, of
Gibbings Grove, co. Cork, and d. 21 Feb. 1865.   (B.P.; Complete
Peerage; Ormerod, iii., 407-16)

2. Sinister background black
Two shields   Dexter, within the circlet of the Order of the Bath and
encircled by the collar of a Knight Grand Cross of the Portuguese Order
of the Tower and Sword with pendant badge flanked on dexter and
sinister respectively by the badges of a Knight Grand Cross of the Most
Honourable Order of the Bath and of the Royal Hanoverian Guelphic
Order, Qly, 1st, Cotton augmented but the field azure, 2nd and 3rd,
Stapleton, 4th, as 1st, but no augmentation, in centre chief the Badge of
Ulster   Sinister, within a circlet of laurel branches, Qly, as dexter,

impaling, Sable on a cross engrailed or five roundels sable a bordure engrailed or (Greville)
Viscountess's coronet   Supporters: On either side a falcon wings expanded proper murally collared and belled gules, supporting a spear proper from which flies a banner, the dexter, azure semy of estoiles argent, and that on the sinister, or   All on a mantle gules and ermine   Cherub's head above and another below
For Caroline, 2nd dau. of William Fulke Greville, who m. 1814, as his second wife, Stapleton, 1st Viscount Combermnere, and d. 25 Jan. 1837.   (Sources, as 1.)

DERBYSHIRE

by

John R. Pierrepont

Trusley 3: For Catherine Coke, 1719
(*Photograph courtesy of Derbyshire Countryside Ltd.*)

INTRODUCTION

As far as I can ascertain nothing has previously been published on the funeral hatchments of Derbyshire; to remedy this I was already engaged in photographing and recording them when I was asked by Mr. Summers to check the Derbyshire section of his records for his national survey. I was delighted to do this for a double check was thereby provided, both as to location and detail. Our lists agreed on the whole; three on his list have disappeared and 11 have not come to light.

Out of some 264 churches in Derbyshire only 35 have (or until recently had) hatchments. The total number recorded since the survey began is 90, the church with the largest number being Trusley which has eight. Derby Cathedral comes second with seven and is followed by Melbourne with six. The earliest is that of Penelope Wright, née Legh (1684) at Great Longstone, and the latest that of Alfred Curzon, 4th Baron Scarsdale (1916) at Kedleston. Of the total number of one hundred hatchments, one is 17th century, 29 are 18th century, 69 are 19th century, and one is 20th century. Apart from those in churches, there are six in a private house, two in a village hall, one in Hardwick Hall and one in Bakewell Museum. There may still be others, and if there are I will be pleased to be told about them. A few are in a shocking condition, but most are in a reasonable state of repair and some have been restored quite recently.

All the hatchments have been identified as to family, but I have not been able to tie three down to a specific individual and I am not absolutely certain as to the attribution of a further three. There are several quarterings which I have not so far been able to identify and will be pleased to hear from anyone who is able to throw light upon them and if possible show how the family concerned acquired them. The heraldry on the hatchments is not by any means always correct, but usually near enough, when examined with pedigree in hand, to enable one to decide which family it is intended for. There is,

however, one gross error on a Sitwell hatchment in Renishaw
Hall, where the hatchment of Sir Sitwell Reresby Sitwell, 3rd
Bt. shows in pretence the arms of Murray, Earls of Dunmore,
with five Murray quarterings. The coat should have been that
of Hely Hutchinson, for Sir Sitwell's wife was the daughter of
a brother of the 3rd Earl of *Donoughmore*. Again with regard to
the Sitwell hatchments it will be noticed that in one case the
field of the Sitwell coat is 'barry of eight or and argent', while
in the rest it is 'barry of eight or and vert'. I do not think this
is a mistake, for George Sitwell (1600-1667) had two grants
of arms. The first by Sir Edward Bysshe in 1647, giving 'barry
or and argent', the second by Sir Edward Walker in 1660
giving 'barry or and vert'.

The earliest hatchment, that of Penelope Wright in Great
Longstone church, provides an interesting example of early
differencing. The impaled coat of Legh is Venables with 'a
bend gobony or and gules over all'. This was done in the 13th
century by a Venables who took his mother's name of Legh.
In more recent times a Heathcote on changing his name to
Rodes (see Barlborough) just added the gold crossed roundels
of the Heathcote coat to that of the Rodes coat.

Finally, apart from the hatchments, there are some 14
armorial panels in the county. The one in Mugginton church
is particularly interesting. It shows the arms of Hugh Radcliffe
and has an inscription which reads like an 18th-century adver-
tisement, stating that Mr. Radcliffe made hats for Charles I
and his family. He also left a small library to the church;
the bookcase is still there but the books have long since
disappeared. Two of these panels are probably funeral escutcheons, 15½ in. by 15½ in., showing the Diocese of Lichfield
impaling Lonsdale. One is at St Luke's, Derby, and the other
is in private possession at Tideswell. John Lonsdale was
Bishop of Lichfield from 1843 to 1868, in which year he died.
There was in St Alkmund's church, Derby, about 20 years
ago a similar panel with the arms of the Archbishop of
Armagh. This church has now been demolished. According
to Robert Simpson's *History and Antiquities of Derby*, 1826, St
Alkmund's also at one time had four hatchments, and he gives
details of them on page 322 of Vol. 1.

John R. Pierrepont,
4 Wye Bank Grove, Bakewell

ALDERWASLEY

1. Dexter background black

Qly, 1st, Sable a fess between three cinquefoils or (Hurt), 2nd, Gules a wolf passant argent (Lowe), 3rd, Azure a hart trippant argent (Lowe), 4th, Argent a bugle horn between three crescents sable each charged with a bezant (Fawne), impaling, Argent on a bend gules three stags' heads cabossed argent (Norman)

Crest: A hart trippant proper, attired, membered and vulned in the flank with an arrow or   Mantling: Gules and argent   Motto: Resurgam

For Francis Hurt, J.P., D.L., who m. 1829, Cecilia Emily, 5th dau. of Richard Norman, of Melton Mowbray, and d. 1 Apr. 1861.   (B.L.G. 5th ed.)

AULT HUCKNALL

1. Dexter 3/4 background black

Two oval shields   Dexter, within the Garter, Qly, 1st and 4th, Sable three bucks' heads cabossed argent attired or (Cavendish), 2nd and 3rd, Per bend embattled argent and gules (Boyle)   Sinister, Qly, 1st and 4th, Qly argent and gules, in the second and third quarters a fret or, over all on a bend sable three escallops argent (Spencer), 2nd and 3rd, Sable a lion rampant argent, on a canton argent a cross gules (Churchill), impaling, Qly, 1st, Gules on a bend argent three trefoils slipped vert (Hervey), 2nd, England, 3rd, qly, i. Gules on a bend between six cross crosslets fitchy argent the Augmentation of Flodden (Howard), ii. Chequy or and azure (Warren), iii. Gules a lion rampant or (Fitzalan), iv. Qly per pale indented or and azure on a bend azure between two eagles displayed or a fret between two martlets or (Audley), 4th, Gules two lions passant in pale argent (for Felton)

Duke's coronet   Crest: A snake nowed proper   Mantle: Gules and ermine   Motto: Cavendo tutus   Supporters: Two bucks proper attired or, each gorged with a chaplet of roses argent seeded gules

For William, 5th Duke of Devonshire, K.G., who m. 1st, 1774, Georgiana, dau. of John, Earl Spencer, and 2nd, 1809, Elizabeth, dau. of Frederick Augustus, 4th Earl of Bristol, and d. 29 July 1811.   (B.P. 1949 ed.)

BAKEWELL Museum

1. All black background

Argent on a fess azure three buckles or (Leslie)

Crest: A griffin's head couped proper langued gules   Motto: Grip
fast   Supporters: Two griffins sejant erect proper winged or langued
gules
Probably for Col. Charles Leslie, 5th son of John Leslie, Baron of
Balquhain, who m. 1836, Dorothea Eyre, of Hassop, Countess of
Newburgh, and d. 10 Jan. 1870. She d. 22 Nov. 1853.   (B.P. 1949
ed.)

BARLBOROUGH
1. All black background
Qly, 1st and 4th, Argent a lion passant guardant in bend gules between
two acorns azure, all between two cotises sable ermined argent, all
between six roundels vert each charged with a cross or (Rodes), 2nd,
Argent a chevron between three cross crosslets sable (Cachehors), 3rd,
Argent three chaplets gules (Lassells)
Crests: Dexter, A cubit arm holding a branch of oak leaves fructed
proper   Sinister, From a mural coronet argent a roundel vert
charged with a cross or between two wings argent   Mantling: Gules
and argent   Motto: Robur meum Deus   Below the shield stalks
of corn in saltire issuing from an escallop
For the Rev. Cornelius Heathcote Reaston Rodes, who m. 1825, Anna
Maria Harriet, dau. of William Gossip, of Hatfield, and d. 22 Feb. 1844,
aged 52.   (B.L.G. 5th ed.; M.I.)

2. All black background
On a lozenge   Qly, 1st, Ermine a lion passant guardant in bend or
between two acorns azure, all between two cotises sable ermined argent
(Rodes), 2nd, Gules a chevron vair between three eagles displayed or
(Wilmer), 3rd, Ermine on a chevron gules between three rudders proper
three cinquefoils or (Reaston), 4th, Sable ermined argent on a chevron
engrailed or three cinquefoils azure (Hatfield)
Probably for Anna Maria Harriet, widow of the Rev. Cornelius
Heathcote Reaston Rodes, d. 16 Feb. 1849, aged 56, since they left no
children, and Wilmer and Hatfield are quarterings of the Gossip
family.   (P.R.)

BARROW-ON-TRENT
1. Dexter background black
Qly of 16, 1st and 16th, Azure semy-de-lys a lion rampant or
(Beaumont), 2nd, Sable three garbs argent (Comyn), 3rd, Gules seven
mascles, three, three and one or (Quincy), 4th, Gules a cinquefoil
ermine (Leicester), 5th, Gules a pale argent (Grandmesnil), 6th, Sable a
lion rampant crowned argent (de Galloway), 7th, Or an inescutcheon
within a tressure flory counter-flory gules (David, Earl of Huntingdon),
8th, Azure six garbs, three, two and one argent (Meschines), 9th, Sable a
wolf's head erased argent (Lupus), 10th, Gules a lion rampant vair
(Everingham), 11th, Azure a fess between three cinquefoils argent

(Maureward), 12th, Vairy argent and sable a fess gules (Bracebridge),
13th, Beaumont, 14th, Argent a maunch sable a crescent gules for
difference (Hastings), 15th, Azure an eagle displayed within a bordure
argent (Tufton), impaling, Argent on a bend sable three popinjays or
collared gules (Curzon)
Crest: On a chapeau azure semy-de-lys or turned up ermine a lion
passant or   Mantling: Gules and argent   Motto: Requiescat
pace
For John Beaumont, who m. 1825, Mary Elizabeth, 3rd dau. of
Nathaniel, 2nd Baron Scarsdale, and d. 11 Mar. 1834.   (Burke's
Commoners, IV, 206)

BRADLEY

1. All black background
On a lozenge surrounded by floriated gilt decoration
Vairy argent and sable (Meynell)   In pretence: Qly, 1st and 4th,
Argent a chevron between three escallops sable (Littleton), 2nd and 3rd,
Or three bars gules (Poyntz)
Motto: In coelo salus   Skull below
For Elizabeth, dau. and heir of Edward Littleton, who m. as his 2nd
wife, Godfrey Meynell, of Bradley, and was bur. 22 May
1726.   (B.L.G. 1937 ed.; P.R.)

CALKE

1. All black background
On a lozenge surrounded by gilt scrollwork and surmounted by a
cherub's head   Qly, 1st and 4th, Azure a lion rampant argent
(Crewe), 2nd and 3rd, Argent a lion rampant within a bordure engrailed
sable (Harpur), over all the Badge of Ulster, impaling, Sable a lion
passant or and in chief three bezants (Hawkins)
Motto: Resurgam
For Ann, dau. of Isaac Hawkins, who m. 1792, Sir Henry Harpur, 7th
Bt. (who took the name of Crewe), and d. 20 Mar. 1827. He d. 7 Feb.
1818.   (B.P. 1939 ed.)

2. Dexter background black
Qly, as 1., with Badge of Ulster, impaling, Sable three mascles or
(Whitaker)
Crests: Dexter, From a ducal coronet or a lion's gamb erect
argent   Sinister, A boar passant proper   Mantling: Gules and
argent   Motto: Degeneranti genus opprobrium
For Sir George Crewe, 8th Bt., who m. 1819, Jane, eldest dau. of the
Rev. Thomas Whitaker, of Mendham, Norfolk, and d. 9 Jan. 1844. She
d. 10 Feb. 1880.   (B.P. 1939 ed.)

3. Dexter background black
Qly, as 1., with Badge of Ulster, impaling, Qly, 1st and 4th, Or three
bars nebuly gules (Lovell), 2nd and 3rd, Argent three cocks in pale
gules between two flaunches sable (Badcock)
Crests: Dexter, as 2.   Centre, From an Eastern crown a cross
or   Sinister, as 2.   Mantling: Azure and argent   Motto:
Resurgam
For Sir John Harpur Crewe, 9th Bt., who m. 1845, Georgiana Jane
Henrietta Eliza, dau. of Vice-Admiral W. Stanhope Lovell, and d. 1
Mar. 1886. She d. 28 May 1910.   (B.P. 1939 ed.)

CASTLETON
1. Sinister background black
Qly, 1st and 4th, qly i. & iv. Gules three cinquefoils ermine (Hamilton),
ii. & iii. Argent a ship with sails furled sable (Arran), 2nd and 3rd,
Argent a heart gules crowned or, on a chief azure three molets argent
(Douglas)   In pretence: Argent a fess gules between three
horseshoes sable (Farran)
Motto: Not lost but gone before   Cherub's head above shield
For Frances Mary, sister of the Rev. Frederick Farran, vicar of Castleton
1780-1817, who m. Capt. George James Hamilton, and d.
1820.   (Derbyshire Arch. Jour., Vol. 77)

CHAPEL-EN-LE-FRITH
1. Dexter background black
Qly, 1st and 4th, Or a buglehorn sable stringed vert between three roses
gules barbed and seeded proper (Bagshawe), 2nd and 3rd, Gules a
chevron ermine between three eagles close or (Child), impaling, Qly,
1st, Azure three well-tops in masonry or (Caldwell), 2nd, Vert a lion
rampant argent langued gules (Hume), 3rd, Argent three popinjays vert
beaked and legged gules (Pepdie), 4th, Gules three cinquefoils ermine
(Hamilton)
Crest: A dexter cubit arm erect the hand proper holding a buglehorn
sable stringed vert   Mantling: Gules and argent   Motto: Forma
flos fama flatus
For Samuel Bagshawe, of Ford Hall, who m. Catherine, dau. of Sir John
Caldwell, Bt., of Castle Caldwell, co. Fermanagh, and d. 16 Aug.
1762.   (B.L.G. 1937 ed.)

2. Dexter background black
Qly, 1st and 4th, Qly gules and vert an eagle displayed holding in the
beak a slip of oak fructed or (Greaves), 2nd, Argent a chevron engrailed
between three trefoils slipped sable (Clay), 3rd, Sable ten elm leaves
erect five and five between three bars engrailed or (Elmsall)   In
pretence: Qly, 1st, Bagshawe, 2nd, Child, 3rd, Gules two bars argent
(Foxlowe), 4th, Azure three molets argent within a double tressure flory
counter-flory or (Murray)

Crest: On a mount vert a stag trippant or holding in his mouth a slip of oak vert   Mantling: Gules and argent   Motto: In veritate triumpho

For Henry Marwood Greaves, of Hesley Hall, Notts, who m. 1829, Mary Catherine Anne, dau. of the Rev. William Bagshawe, of Ford Hall, and d. 10 Mar. 1859.   (B.L.G. 1937 ed.)

CHURCH GRESLEY

1. All black background

Vairy ermine and gules, on a crescent or a label sable for difference (Gresley)   To dexter of main shield, Gresley differenced, impaling, Gresley, no difference marks, A.B1.   To sinister of main shield, Gresley differenced, impaling, Argent a lion rampant gules between eight fleurs-de-lys azure (Thorpe), D.B1.

Crest: A lion passant ermine langued and collared gules   Motto: Spes mea Christus

For the Rev. William Gresley, who m. 1st, 1798, Louisa Jane (d. 26 Apr. 1806), dau. of Sir Nigel Gresley, 6th Bt., and 2nd, 1811, Mary (d. 19 July 1869), dau. of Thomas Thorp, of Overseale, Leics, and d. 3 Oct. 1829.   (B.P. 1949 ed.)

2. Dexter background black

Qly of twelve, 1st and 12th, Vairy ermine and gules (Gresley), 2nd, Sable a lion rampant argent (Wasteney), 3rd, Argent a lion rampant between three cross crosslets fitchy gules (Bowyer), 4th, Azure three spades or handled argent (Knipersley), 5th, Azure two bars and in chief two roundels argent (Venables), 6th, Azure a bend or a bordure ermine (Grosvenor), 7th, Azure six martlets three, two and one or (Bucknall), 8th, Argent on a bend cotised gules three roundels argent (Haywood), 9th, Argent a grenade sable fired proper (Stonylowe), 10th, Ermine on a fess gules three bezants (Milward), 11th, Gules a pile between four leopards' heads or, over all a fess azure (Garway), impaling, Qly of six, 1st and 6th, Sable a fess ermine between three crescents or (Coventry), 2nd and 5th, Argent a fess between two chevrons gules and three gouttes two in chief and one in base gules (Pitches), 3rd, Argent three snakes embowed erect two and one vert (Teague), 4th, Argent three lions rampant gules (Bellhouse), the Badge of Ulster over impalement line

Crest: A lion passant ermine langued and collared gules   Mantling: Gules and argent   Motto: Resurgam

For Sir Roger Gresley, 8th Bt., who m. 1821, Sophia Catherine, youngest dau. of George William, 7th Earl of Coventry, and d.s.p. 12 Oct. 1837.   (B.P. 1949 ed.)

3. Dexter background black

Qly of eight, 1st and 8th, Vairy ermine and gules (Gresley), 2nd, Sable a lion rampant argent armed, langued and collared gules (Wasteney), 3rd, Vert a tree argent fructed or (Morewood), 4th, Azure three ducal

coronets or a bordure argent (Lee), 5th, Azure three quatrefoils argent
(Vincent), 6th, Argent a lion rampant between three cross crosslets
fitchy gules (Bowyer), 7th, Ermine a saltire gules (Wynne), in fess point
the Badge of Ulster, impaling, Argent a doubleheaded eagle displayed
sable charged on the breast with an escutcheon gules (Reid)
Crest: A lion passant ermine, armed, langued and collared
gules   Mantling: Gules and argent, edged or   Mottoes: In te
Dne speravi   In aeternum non confundar
For the Rev. Sir William Nigel Gresley, 9th Bt., who m. 1831, Georgina
Anne, 2nd dau. of George Reid, and d. 3 Sept. 1847.   (B.P. 1949
ed.)

4. Sinister background black

Vairy ermine and gules (Gresley), impaling, Or a fess dancetty sable
(Vavasour), a crescent for difference over line of impalement
Motto: In te Domine speravi   An anchor within a circle above
shield   On a wood panel
For Penelope, dau. of the Rev. Marmaduke Vavasour, Vicar of Ashby-
de-la-Zouch, who m. 1849, the Rev. John Morewood Gresley, Rector of
Seale, and d. 22 Feb. 1858.   (B.P. 1949 ed.; Vicar)

CLOWNE

1. Dexter background black

Qly, 1st and 4th, Qly sable and or in the first quarter a lion passant
argent langued gules (Bowdon), 2nd, Gules a bordure ermine (   ),
3rd, Argent on a chevron gules three bezants (Erdeswick), impaling, Or
three bars nebuly sable (Blount)
Crests: Dexter, A heron's head erased or   Sinister, From a ducal
coronet or a demi-eagle displayed proper   Mantling: Gules and
argent   Motto: Vanus est honor
For Henry Bowdon, of Southgate House, who m. Henrietta Matilda, 4th
dau. of Michael Blount, of Mapledurham, Oxon, and d. 3 May
1875.   (B.L.G. 1937 ed.)

2. All black background

Qly, 1st and 4th, Qly sable and or, in the first quarter a lion statant
argent (Bowden), 2nd, Gules a bordure ermine (   ), 3rd, Argent on
a chevron gules five bezants (Erdeswick)
Crests, mantling and motto: As 1. Stencilled in one corner, J. Castle of
Newark and Worksop
Probably for Henry Bowdon, uncle of 1.   (Glover's History and
Gazetteer)

DERBY Cathedral

1. All black background

Or three crescents between the points of each an estoile gules, a canton
azure (Bateman), impaling, Or on a bend azure between two wolves'

heads erased sable langued gules three dolphins or (Osborne)   In
pretence (over impalement line): Azure a cross vairy or and azure
between four molets of six points or (Hacker)
Crest: A crescent, between the horns an estoile gules, all between a pair
of wings or   Mantling: Gules and argent   Motto: Mors janua
vitae
For Hugh Bateman, of Hartington, who m. 1st, 1718, Elizabeth (d. July,
1723), dau. and eventual co-heir of John Osborne, of Derby, and 2nd,
1723, Elizabeth, dau. of Samuel Hacker, of Duffield, and d. 24 Nov.
1777.   (Burke's Family Records)

2. Dexter background black
Qly, 1st and 4th, Bateman, 2nd and 3rd, Osborne   In pretence:
Qly, 1st and 4th, Gules a cross argent a canton or (Keelinge), 2nd and
3rd, Argent six lions rampant three, two and one sable (Savage)
Crest and mantling: As 1.   Motto: In coelo quies
For Richard Bateman, of Wheat Hall, who m. 1791, Elizabeth, only
child and heiress of the Rev. Thomas Keelinge, of Uttoxeter, by Mary,
his wife, dau. of the Rev. John Savage, and d. 29 Mar.
1821.   (Source, as 1.)

3. All black background
On a lozenge   Argent on a chevron between three chambers in fess
pointing to the dexter sable fired proper a chevron ermine (Chambers),
impaling, Argent a cinquefoil azure, on a chief gules a lion passant
guardant or (Rolleston)
Motto: In coelo quies
For Dorothy, dau. of the Rev. John Rolleston, Rector of Aston, who m.
the Rev. William Chambers, D.D., Rector of Achester, Northants, and d.
1st Nov. 1801.   (Jewitt's Reliquary)

4. Dexter background black
Ermine three copper cakes proper, on a chief gules a chamber or
(Chambers), impaling, Barry of six or and ermine a lion rampant sable
langued gules (Bagnold)
Crest: Within a mountain vert a man working in a copper mine holding
a pickaxe elevated proper, his cap, shirt, drawers and hose argent, shoes
sable, the planet Venus rising behind the mountain or   Mantling:
Gules and argent   Motto: Mors janua vitae
For Thomas Chambers, who m. Margaret (Bagnold) and d. 10 Dec.
1726.   (M.I.)

5. All black background
On a lozenge surmounted by a skull
Arms: As 4.
Motto: In coelo salus

For Margaret, widow of Thomas Chambers, d. 23 Apr.
1735.   (M.I.)

6. All black backgound
Gules three crescents and a canton or (Coke of Trusley)
Crest: The sun in splendour or   Mantling: Gules and
argent   Motto: Mihi coelum portus
For Daniel Parker Coke, Barrister, who d. 6 Dec. 1825, or his father,
Thomas Coke, d. 15 Nov. 1776.   (M.I. to father bears paternal arms
only)

7. All black background
Argent a chevron between three eagles displayed gules (Francis)   In
pretence: Argent a lion rampant within a bordure engrailed sable
(Harpur)
Crest: A falcon rising or, in its beak a grape vine   Mantling: Gules
and argent   Motto: Mors janua vitae
For Henry Francis, who m. Anne, dau. and co-heir of John Harpur, and
d. 4 Jan. 1747.   (Derby School reg.; Nichols' Leicestershire)

DOVERIDGE
1. Dexter background black
Qly, 1st and 4th, Sable three bucks' heads cabossed argent attired or
(Cavendish), 2nd and 3rd, Argent two bends the upper azure the lower
gules (Bradshaw), over all the Badge of Ulster   In pretence: Gules
a fess between three lions passant or (Cooper)
Baron's coronet   Crest: A snake nowed proper   Mantling: Gules
and ermine   Motto: Cavendo tutus   Supporters: Two stags, the
dexter, per fess indented gules and sable, the sinister, proper, gorged
with a chaplet of roses, alternately argent and azure, both attired or
For Richard, 2nd Baron Waterpark, who m. 1789, Juliana, eldest dau.
and co-heir of Thomas Cooper, of Cooper's Hill, and Mullimast Castle,
co. Kildare, and d. 1 June 1830.   (B.P. 1949 ed.)

2. All black background
On a lozenge   Qly, 1st and 4th, Cavendish, 2nd, Gules a chevron
ermine between three pineapples or (Pyne), 3rd, Bradshaw, in chief the
Badge of Ulster   In pretence: Cooper
Baroness's coronet   Supporters: As 1., but both attired and unguled
or
For Juliana, widow of Richard, 2nd Baron Waterpark, d. 11 Oct.
1847.   (B.P. 1949 ed.)

3. Dexter background black
Qly, 1st and 4th, Cavendish, with bordure or, 2nd and 3rd, Bradshaw,
impaling, Qly, 1st, Argent three bendlets gules, in sinister chief a
crescent sable for difference (Anson), 2nd, Ermine three cats-a-mountain

passant in pale sable (Adams), 3rd, Azure three salmon naiant in pale proper (Sambrooke), 4th, Sable a bend between three spearheads argent (Carrier)
Baron's coronet   Mantling: Gules and ermine   Motto: Cavendo tutus   Supporters: As 2.
For Henry Manners, 3rd Baron Waterpark, who m. 1837, Elizabeth Jane, dau. of Thomas, 1st Viscount Anson, and d. 31 Mar. 1863.   (B.P. 1949 ed.)

EGGINGTON

1. All black background
Or four chevronels gules, in dexter chief the Badge of Ulster (Every)
Crest: A unicorn's head erased argent armed or   Mantling: Gules and or   Motto: Mors janua vitae
Possibly for the Rev. Sir John Every, 7th Bt., who m. 1767, Dorothy Pakeman, and d.s.p. 29 June 1779.   (B.P. 1949 ed.)
(This hatchment was recorded in 1954, but has since disappeared)

2. Dexter background black
Qly, 1st and 4th, Or four chevronels gules (Every), 2nd and 3rd, Azure a bezant between three crowns or and a bordure argent (Leigh), over all the Badge of Ulster
Crest: A demi-unicorn rampant argent, crined, hoofed, tailed, horned and bearded or   Mantling: Gules and or   Motto: Mors janua vitae
Probably for Sir Edward Every, 8th Bt., who m. 1776, Mary, dau. of Edward Morley, of Horsley, and d. 4 Jan. 1786.   (B.P. 1949 ed.)

3. All black background
Qly, 1st and 4th, Sable a chevron between three pickaxes argent (Mosley), 2nd, Or a fess between three eagles displayed sable (Mosley), 3rd, Gules a wolf passant argent (Lowe), over all a molet gules for difference, impaling, Vert/Azure a lion rampant or langued gules (?Morley)
Crest: An eagle displayed ermine langued gules, on its breast a molet gules   Mantling: Sable and argent   Motto: Mos legem regit
For Ashton Nicholas Mosley, of Park Hill, who m. 1790, Mary, dau. of Edward Morley, formerly wife of Sir Edward Every, 8th Bt., and d. 2 Apr. 1830.   (B.P. 1949 ed.)

ELVASTON

1. All black background
Two shields   Dexter, within Order of the Grand Cross of Hanover, with badge pendent, Qly ermine and gules (Stanhope)   Sinister, as dexter, within pretence, Argent a chevron within a tressure flory counter-flory gules (Fleming)

Earl's coronet   Motto: A Deo et rege   Supporters: Dexter, A
talbot guardant argent gutty sable   Sinister, A wolf or ermined
sable   Each gorged with a chaplet of oak vert fructed or   All on
a mantle gules and ermine
For Charles, 3rd Earl of Harrington, G.C.H., who m. 1779, Jane (d. 3
Feb. 1824), dau. and co-heir of Sir John Fleming, Bt., of Brompton Park,
and d. 5 Sept. 1829.   (B.P. 1949 ed.)

2. All black background
Qly, 1st and 4th, Qly ermine and gules a crescent for difference
(Stanhope), 2nd and 3rd, Per pale azure and gules a chevron
counterchanged between three bucks trippant or (Green)
Earl's coronet   Crest: From a tower azure a demi-lion issuant or
crowned gules, between the paws a grenade proper   Motto and
supporters: As 1.
Inscribed on frame 'Seymour Sydney Hyde, 6th Earl of Harrington, Born
27th Sep. 1845. Died 22nd February 1866.'

3. All black background
On a lozenge   Qly ermine and gules (Stanhope), impaling, Or a
chevron and in dexter chief a trefoil slipped sable (Foote)
Countess's coronet   Supporters: As 1.   All on a mantle gules
and ermine
For Maria, dau. of Samuel Foote, who m. Charles, 4th Earl of
Harrington, and d. 27 Dec. 1867.   (B.P. 1949 ed.)

ETWALL
1. All black background
Azure a chevron between three hanks of cotton argent (Cotton)
Crest: A falcon proper, the dexter claw supporting a belt proper buckle
or   Mantling: Gules and argent   Motto: Resurgam
Probably for William Cotton, of Etwall Hall, who d. unm. 4 Nov.
1819.   (B.L.G. 1937 ed.)

2. Dexter background black
Cotton, impaling, Argent two bends between two martlets sable
(Bradshaw)
Crest, mantling and motto: As 1.
For the Rev. Charles Evelyn Cotton, of Etwall Hall, who m. 1828,
Frances Maria, dau. of Francis Bradshaw, of Barton Hall, and d. 3 Mar.
1857.   (B.L.G. 1937 ed.)

3. All black background
On a lozenge   Qly of eight, 1st, Cotton, 2nd, Argent a fess engrailed
sable between three molets gules (Cotton), 3rd, Or an eagle's leg erased
gules, on a chief azure a molet between two roundels argent (Tarbock),
4th, Argent a chevron sable between three laurel leaves vert, a chief

sable (Shabery), 5th, Gules a chevron between three owls or (Sleigh), 6th, Gules three cross crosslets fitchy sable a chief or (Ardern), 7th, Or a fess between three cross crosslets fitchy sable (Ryley), 8th, Or a lion rampant vert (Sutton)   In pretence: Cotton, as 1., impaling, Sleigh For Mary Sleigh, who m. Rowland Cotton, and d. 1761, aged 82.   (B.P. 1949 ed.; Jewitt's Reliquary)

FOREMARK

1. Sinister background black

Azure two bars or, in centre chief the Badge of Ulster (Burdett)   In pretence: Argent a stag's head erased gules, between the attires a pheon all within a bordure embattled azure charged with four buckles or (Coutts)

Two cherubs' heads above

For Sophia, dau. and co-heir of Thomas Coutts, of London, who m. 1793, Sir Francis Burdett, 5th Bt., and d. 12 Jan. 1844.   (B.P. 1949 ed.)

2. All black background

Arms: As 1., but Badge of Ulster in dexter chief

Crest: A lion's head erased sable langued gules   Mantling: Gules and argent   Motto: Cleave fast

For Sir Francis Burdett, 5th Bt., who d. 23 Jan. 1844.   (B.P. 1949 ed.)

3. All black background

Qly, 1st and 4th, Azure two bars or on each three martlets gules (Burdett), 2nd and 3rd, Coutts without buckles on bordure, in centre chief the Badge of Ulster

Crest, mantling and motto: As 2.

For Sir Robert Burdett, 6th Bt., who d. unm. 7 June 1880.   (B.P. 1949 ed.)

HARDWICK Hall

1. All black background

Within the Garter, Qly, 1st and 4th, Sable three bucks' heads cabossed argent attired or (Cavendish), 2nd, Per bend embattled argent and gules (Boyle), 3rd, Chequy or and azure a fess gules (Clifford)

Duke's coronet   Crest: A serpent nowed proper   Mantling: Azure and or   Motto: Cavendo tutus   Supporters: Two bucks proper attired or, each gorged with a garland of roses argent and azure   Pendent below shield are three Orders: centre, the Garter, and on either side the Order of St Alexander Nevski and St Andrew of Russia

For William Spencer, 6th Duke of Devonshire, K.G., K.S.A., K.A.N., who d. unm. 17 Jan. 1858, aged 67.   (B.P. 1949 ed.)

(There is another hatchment for the 6th Duke at Bolton Abbey, Yorkshire)

HEANOR

1. Dexter background black

Azure a chevron engrailed ermine between three scimitars proper, the two in chief erect, the one in base fesswise, on a chief or three martlets gules (Ray)

Crest: An ostrich or, in the beak a horseshoe azure   Mantling: Gules and argent   Motto: Resurgam

Possibly for John Ray, d. 29 Dec. 1867.   (Derbyshire Record Office, Ray papers; P.R.)

HULLAND

1. Dexter background black

Qly of twenty, 1st and 20th, Argent on a mount in base the trunk of an oak with two branches proper hanging thereon the shield of Pallas or from a belt gules (Borough), 2nd, Azure a fess between three talbots' heads erased or (Burton), 3rd, Azure three molets within a bordure or (Burton), 4th, Gules a saltire engrailed argent between four molets or (Hardwick), 5th, Vairy or and gules, on a bordure sable ten martlets argent (Curzon), 6th, Vairy argent and sable a chevron gules (Ashbrook), 7th, Azure an eagle displayed argent beaked and legged gules (Ridware), 8th, Gules crusilly fitchy argent (Faunt de Foston), 9th, Or five bendlets azure (Fundin), 10th, Or fretty sable charged at each intersection with a cross crosslet fitchy argent (Champaigne), 11th, Argent a bend between three roundels two and one sable (Cotton), 12th, Gules three eagles displayed or (Linsey), 13th, obscured by pretence coat, 14th, Argent a fess gules and in chief three molets sable (Flanders), 15th, Argent a chevron between three lozenges sable ermined argent (Shaw), 16th, Or three molets of six points pierced gules (Curtis), 17th, Gules on a bend or three chaplets vert (Stevens), 18th, Azure semy of cinquefoils or (Rodville), 19th, Qly gules and argent four crosses formy counterchanged, on a bordure qly argent and gules six roundels counterchanged (Alt)   In pretence: Qly of six, 1st and 6th, Sable three horseshoes and a label of three points argent (Smithson), 2nd, Azure a chevron or between three windmill sails crossways argent (Milnes), 3rd, Azure on a fess cotised argent three leopards' faces gules (Lee), 4th, Argent a chevron gules between three fountains (Sykes), 5th, Ermine on a chief sable two molets argent (Raynor)

Crest: An eagle reguardant wings displayed on a mount proper, supporting with dexter foot a shield as in the arms   Motto: Mors janua vitae

For Thomas Borough, of Castlefield, who m. 1788, Jane, only dau. of William Smithson, of Ledstone Park, Ferrybridge, Yorks, and d. 29 May 1838.   (B.L.G. 1937 ed.; Derby Mercury)

KEDLESTON
1. Dexter background black
Argent on a bend sable three popinjays or collared beaked and legged gules, in chief the Badge of Ulster (Curzon), impaling, Gules on a chevron between three wolves' heads erased close argent three trees eradicated proper fructed or (Colyear)
Baron's coronet   Crest: A basilisk wings elevated tail nowed or   Mantling: Gules and argent   Motto: Recte et sauviter   Supporters: Dexter, the figure of Prudence, a woman habited argent mantled azure, holding in the left hand a spear entwined with a snake proper   Sinister, the figure of Liberality, a woman habited argent mantled purpure holding a cornucopia proper   Nova Scotia badge pendent below
For Nathaniel, 1st Baron Scarsdale, who m. 1750, Caroline, eldest dau. of Charles, 2nd Earl of Portmore, and d. 6 Dec. 1804.   (B.P. 1949 ed.)

2. Dexter two-thirds black
Qly of twelve, 1st, Curzon, with Badge of Ulster in dexter base, 2nd, Argent a fret sable (Vernon), 3rd, Argent a lion rampant sable (Ludlow), 4th, Gules a lion rampant or a bordure argent (Grey), 5th, Or a lion rampant gules (Cherleton), 6th, Or a lion's gamb erased paleways gules (Powys), 7th, Azure fleuretty a lion rampant argent (Holland), 8th, Gules three lions passant or a bordure argent (Woodstock), 9th, Or two bars gules in chief three roundels gules (Wake), 10th, Argent on a fess sable three bezants (Penn), 11th, Argent a molet sable (Assheton), 12th, Or a fess dancetty sable (Vavasour), impaling to the dexter, Qly, 1st and 4th, Or fretty gules a canton ermine (Noel), 2nd, Sable a chevron between three leopards' faces or (Wentworth), 3rd, Gules on a chief azure three martlets or (Lovelace), and impaling to the sinister, Gules two swords in saltire proper between four crosses formy argent (de Wattines)
Baron's coronet   Crest: A popinjay rising or collared beaked and legged gules   Supporters and badge: As 1.   Mantle: Gules and ermine   Motto: Recte et sauviter
For Nathaniel, 2nd Baron Scarsdale, who m. 1st, 1777, Sophia Susanna, 3rd dau. of Edward, 1st Viscount Wentworth, and 2nd, 1798, Felicité Anne Josephe de Wattines, and d. 26 Jan. 1837.   (B.P. 1949 ed.)

3. All black background
On a lozenge   Curzon, no Badge of Ulster, impaling, de Wattines
Baroness's coronet   Supporters: As 1.
For Felicité, 2nd wife of Nathaniel, 2nd Baron Scarsdale, d. 16 Dec. 1850.   (B.P. 1949 ed.)

4. All black background
Curzon, as 1.
Baron's coronet   Crest: A popinjay rising or   Motto: As 2.   Supporters and badge: As 1.

For Nathaniel, 3rd Baron Scarsdale, who d. unm. 12 Nov.
1856.   (B.P. 1949 ed.)

5. All black background

Curzon, as 3., impaling, Qly, 1st and 4th, Or a popinjay proper
(Senhouse), 2nd and 3rd, Ermine three bends azure, on a chief or three
martlets sable (Pocklington)
Baron's coronet   Crest and motto: As 2.   Supporters and badge:
As 1.
For Alfred, 4th Baron Scarsdale, Rector of Kedleston 1855-1916, who m.
1856, Blanche, 2nd dau. of Joseph Pocklington Senhouse, of Netherhall,
Cumberland, and d. 23 Mar. 1916.   (B.P. 1949 ed.)

KIRK HALLAM

1. All black background

Gules three lions gambs erased or (Newdigate), impaling, Azure a
buck's head cabossed argent (Legge)
Crest: A fleur-de-lys argent   Mantling: Gules and
argent   Mottoes: (on scroll above crest) Foyall loyall   (below
shield) Confide recte agens
For Francis Newdigate, who m. 1820, Barbara Maria, dau. of George,
3rd Earl of Dartmouth, and d. 21 May 1862.   (B.L.G. 5th ed.; Visit.
of England and Wales)

LITTLEOVER

1. Dexter background black

Ermine three roundels vert each charged with a cross or
(Heathcote)   In pretence: Qly, 1st and 4th, Argent a chevron azure
between three moles sable (Twisleton), 2nd and 3rd, Gules six gouttes,
three, two and one argent, on a chief or a griffin passant sable
(Cockshutt)
Crest: Out of a mural coronet azure a roundel vert charged with a cross
or, between two wings displayed ermine   Mantling: Gules and
argent   Motto: Mors janua vitae
For Bache Heathcote, who m. Mary, only child of Josias Cockshutt, and
d. 31 Jan. 1826.   (M.I.; E. D. Heathcote, Family of Heathcote)

LONGFORD

1. Dexter background black

Per pale gules and azure three eagles displayed argent (Coke), impaling,
Gules three escallops argent (Keppel)
Earl's coronet   Crest: On a chapeau azure and ermine an ostrich
proper in its beak a horseshoe or   Mantling: Gules and
argent   Motto: Resurgam   Supporters: Two ostriches proper,
the dexter ducally gorged azure stringed gules, the sinister ducally
gorged gules stringed azure

For Thomas, 1st Earl of Leicester, who m. 2nd, 1822, Anne Amelia, dau.
of William, 4th Earl of Albemarle, and d. 30 June 1842.   (B.P.
1949 ed.)
(There is another hatchment for Lord Leicester at Tittleshall, Norfolk)

2. Sinister background black
Or three helms affronté proper (Ellice), impaling, two coats per pale,
Coke and Keppel
Countess's coronet
For Anne, formerly Countess of Leicester, who m. 2nd, 1843, the Rt.
Hon. Edward Ellice, M.P., and d. 22 July 1844.   (B.P. 1949 ed.)

GREAT LONGSTONE
1. All black background
Argent on a chevron sable three quatrefoils or (Eyre), impaling, Sable a
bend argent, in the sinister chief a tower tripletowered or (Plunkett)
Crest: An armed leg couped at the thigh qly argent and
sable   Mantling: Gules and argent   Skull in base
For Rowland Eyre, of Hassop, who m. Elizabeth, dau. of Luke, 3rd Earl
of Fingall, and d. 12 Mar. 1728/9.   (B.E.P.; Jewitt's Reliquary, Vol.
X)

2. All black background
Eyre   In pretence: Vert a chevron between three pheons or
(Holman)
Crest: An armed leg couped at the thigh sable outlined
or   Mantling: Gules and argent   Motto: In coelo
quies   Skull and crossbones in base
For Thomas Eyre, who m. Mary Holman, and was bur. 27 Feb.
1749.   (Jewitt's Reliquary, Vol. X; Eyres of Hassop, R. Meredith)

3. Dexter background black
Argent on a chevron sable three cinquefoils or (Eyre), impaling, Qly, 1st
and 4th, Argent a chevron gules between three fleurs-de-lys azure
(Bellasis), 2nd and 3rd, Argent a pale engrailed endorsed sable
(Bellasis)
Crest and mantling: As 1.   Motto: In coelo quies
For Thomas Eyre, of Hassop, who m. 1776, Mary, dau. of Thomas, 1st
Earl Fauconberg, and d. 26 Mar. 1792.   (Sources, as 1.)

4. All black background
On a lozenge surmounted by a skull
Sable on a chevron engrailed between three unicorns' heads erased or
three spearheads sable (Wright), impaling, Azure two bars argent, over
all a bend compony or and gules (Legh)
For Penelope, dau. of Thomas Legh, who m. William Wright, and d. 22
Apr. 1684.   (Longstone Records, G. T. Wright, 1906)

5. All black background
On a lozenge surmounted by a skull
Sable on a chevron engrailed between three unicorns' heads erased or three spearheads sable (Wright), impaling, Argent a fret sable and a canton gules (Vernon)
Motto: Mors janua vitae
For Ann, dau. of Sir Thomas Vernon, of Coleman Street, London, who m. Thomas Wright, and was bur. 6 Mar. 1707/8.   (Wright family)

LULLINGTON, Village Hall
1. All black background
Azure a lion rampant or a label of three points gules the whole width of the shield (Colvile), impaling, Gules a fess within a bordure engrailed ermine (Acton)
Crest: On a chapeau gules and ermine a lion statant tail extended argent, gorged with a label of three points gules   Mantling: Gules and argent   Motto: Mors janua vitae
For Richard Colvile, of Newton Colvile, who m. Elizabeth, dau. of Nathanial Acton, of Bramford Hall, Suffolk, and d. 11 Apr. 1784.   (B.L.G. 1937 ed.)

2. Dexter background black
Qly of sixteen, 1st and 16th, Azure a lion rampant or a label of five points gules the whole width of the shield (Colvile), 2nd, Or three chess rooks gules (de Marisco), 3rd, Gules three trowels argent (de Lisle), 4th, Chequy or and azure, a label of five points gules (Warren), 5th, Argent a horse trotting sable caparisoned or (Rustyn), 6th, as 1st, 7th, as 4th, 8th, Azure three griffins passant in pale or (Wythe), 9th, Azure a fess between six cross crosslets or (St Omer), 10th and 11th, obscured by shield in pretence, 12th, Azure three buckles or (Carter), 13th, Argent on a bend sable in a chief a bezant (Pinchbeck), 14th, Argent a fret sable, on a chief azure a lion passant argent (Sarson), 15th, Or on a fess between three molets of six points sable three roundels argent (Waite)   In pretence: Qly, 1st and 4th, Or a lion rampant sable between eight fleurs-de-lys gules (Bonell), 2nd, Sable three church bells argent a canton ermine (Porter), 3rd, Argent on a chevron azure between three roses gules three fleurs-de-lys argent (Coape)
Crest: As 1.   Mantling: Azure and or   Motto: In Deo credo
For Sir Charles Henry Colvile, of Duffield Hall, who m. 1813, Harriet Anne, dau. of Thomas Porter Bonell, heiress to the families of Porter and Coape, by Anne, dau. of Joseph Bradshawe, of Barton Hall, and d. 28 Sept. 1833.   (B.L.G. 1937 ed.)

MATLOCK, St Giles

1. All black background

Sable a chevron vairy or and gules between three maidens' heads couped proper crined or (Wolley)

Crest: A maiden's head proper   Mantling: Gules and argent

On motto scroll: Wolley coat of arms   Skull below   On a wood panel

Unidentified

MELBOURNE

1. All black background

Qly, 1st and 4th, Gules three crescents and a canton or (Coke), 2nd and 3rd, Argent a bend compony gules and argent cotised gules (Leventhorpe)   To dexter of main shield, Coke, impaling, Qly ermine and gules (Stanhope) A.B1.   To sinister of main shield, Coke, impaling, Azure a chevron embattled counter-embattled or (Hale) A.B1.

Crest: The sun in splendour or   Mantling: Gules and argent   Motto: Mors janua vitae

For Thomas Coke, who m. 1st, Mary, dau. of Philip, 2nd Earl of Chesterfield, and 2nd, Mary, dau. of Richard Hale, of King's Walden, and d. 11 May 1727.   (B.L.G. 2nd ed.; B.P. 1875 ed.)

2. All black background

Qly, 1st and 4th, Coke, 2nd and 3rd, Argent a bend compony gules and sable cotised gules (Leventhorpe)

Crest: Arising from a cloud argent the sun in splendour or   Mantling: Gules and argent   Motto: In coelo quies   Skull in base

For George Lewis Coke, who d. 4 Jan. 1750.   (J. T. Coke, Coke of Trusley)

3. Dexter background black

Qly, 1st and 4th, Sable on a fess or ermined sable between three cinquefoils argent two molets sable (Lamb), 2nd and 3rd, Coke, impaling, blank (argent with black arabesques)

Crest: A demi-lion rampant gules holding a molet sable   Mantling: Gules and argent   Motto: Virtute et fide

For George Lamb, son of Peniston, 1st Viscount Melbourne, who m. 1809, Mlle Caroline Rosalie St Jules, and d.s.p. 2 Jan. 1834.   (B.E.P.)

4. All black background

Qly, 1st and 4th, Sable on a fess between three cinquefoils or two molets azure (Lamb), 2nd and 3rd, Coke, impaling, Gules a bend ermine, on a canton or a lion's head erased gules (Milbanke)

Viscount's coronet   Crest: A demi-lion rampant gules holding in dexter paw a molet azure   Motto: As 3.   Supporters: Two lions

rampant gules collared and chained or, each collar charged with two molets sable
For Peniston, 1st Viscount Melbourne, who m. 1769, Elizabeth, only dau. of Sir Ralph Milbanke, 5th Bt., and d. 22 July 1828.   (B.E.P.)

5. All black background
Qly, as 3., with Badge of Ulster at fess point
Viscount's coronet   Crest and motto: As 3.   Supporters: As 4.
For William, 2nd Viscount Melbourne, who m. Caroline, only dau. of Frederick, 3rd Earl of Bessborough, and d. 24 Nov. 1848.   (B.E.P.)

6. Dexter background black
Two oval shields, the dexter overlapping the sinister   Dexter, within the Order of the Bath, Qly, as 3. but fess ermine, over all the Badge of Ulster   Sinister, within an ornamental wreath, Per pale, Azure two conies' heads couped or, and, Or three flowers azure
(Maltzahn)   Badge of Order pendent below
Viscount's coronet   Crest and motto: As 3.   Supporters: As 4.
All on a mantle gules and ermine
For Frederick, 3rd Viscount Melbourne, who m,. 1841, Countess Alexandrine, dau. of Joachim, Count of Maltzahn, and d. 29 Jan. 1853.   (B.E.P.)

MORTON
1. Dexter background black
Azure three turbots argent (Turbutt), impaling, Azure three fleurs-de-lys or (Burrow)
Crest: A sinister arm embowed holding a trident or   Mantling: Gules and argent   Cherub's head above and skull below
For William Turbutt, of Ogston Hall, who m. 1767, Elizabeth, dau. and co-heiress of Benjamin Burrow, rector of Morton, and d. 23 Aug. 1817.   (B.L.G. 5th ed.)

2. Dexter background black
Qly, 1st, Turbutt, 2nd, Ermine on a bend gules three boars' heads couped argent (Driffield), 3rd, Argent ten roundels, four, three, two and one gules a label of five points azure (Babington), 4th, Argent on a cross gules five swans argent (Clarke), impaling, Ermine a chief azure, over all on a bend gules a sword point upwards argent hilt and pommel or (Gladwin)
Crest: indistinguishable   Mantling: Gules and argent   Motto: indistinguishable
For William Turbutt, of Ogston Hall, who m. 1814, Anne, dau. of Major-Gen. Gladwin, of Stubbin Court, and d. 25 Dec. 1836.   (B.L.G. 5th ed.)

OCKBROOK

1. All black background

Sable a chevron argent, in dexter chief a cross crosslet argent (Pares),
impaling, Vert a lion rampant within a bordure engrailed or (Norton)
Crest: A demi-griffin or armed and langued gules   Mantling: Gules
and argent   Motto: Spea mea in Deo   Skull below
For Thomas Pares, of Hopwell Hall, who m. Ann Norton, and d. 21
May 1805, aged 88.   (B.L.G. 1937 ed.)

RADBOURNE

1. Dexter background black

Qly of nine, 1st, Argent a chevron between three crescents gules (Pole),
2nd, Or a stag's head cabossed gules (Hartington), 3rd. Azure a fess
gules between six lozenges sable (Wakebridge), 4th, Argent a pile gules
(Chandos), 5th, Barry of six gules and azure a lion rampant ermine
(Walkelin), 6th, Argent a cinquefoil azure (Moton), 7th, Or three piles
gules a canton vair (Basset), 8th, Argent on a saltire azure five water
bougets or (Sacheverell), 9th, Argent three hares playing bagpipes gules
(Fitzercald), impaling, Or two lions passant azure, on a bordure azure
eight escallops or (Warre)
Crest: A hawk rising proper belled and jessed or   Mantling: Gules
and argent   Motto: In coelo quies   Skull blow
For Sacherverell Chandos-Pole, who m. 1791, Mary, dau. of the Rev.
Henry Ware, D.D., and d. 14 Apr. 1813.   (B.L.G. 1937 ed.)

2. Dexter background black

Qly, 1st and 4th, Pole, 2nd and 3rd, Chandos, impaling, Sable on a fess
or between three eagles' heads couped argent three escallops gules, a
canton vairy gules and ermine (Wilmot)
Crest: A hawk rising proper   Mantling: Gules and argent
For Edward Sacheverell Chandos-Pole, who m. 1819, Anna Maria, dau.
of the Rev. E. S. Wilmot, and d. 19 Jan. 1863.   (B.L.G. 1937 ed.)

3. Dexter background black

Qly, 1st and 4th, Pole, 2nd and 3rd, Chandos, impaling, Qly ermine
and gules, a crescent argent on a crescent sable for difference (Stanhope)
Crest and mantling: As 2.
For Edward Sacheverell Chandos-Pole, who m. 1850, Anna Carolina,
dau. of Leicester, 5th Earl of Harrington, and d. 30 Nov.
1873.   (B.L.G. 1937 ed.)

RENISHAW Hall

1. Sinister background black

Barry of eight or and vert three lions rampant sable (Sitwell), impaling,
Per fess embattled argent and sable six crosses formy counterchanged
(Warnford)

Motto: In coelo quies   Cherub's head at each top corner of
shield   Winged skull in base
For Mary, sister to Col. Warneford, of Warneford Place, who m. Francis
Hurt (who assumed the name and arms of Sitwell), and d. 13 July
1792.   (B.P. 1949 ed.)

2. All black background
Arms: As 1.
Crest: A demi-lion rampant sable holding a shield per pale or and
vert   Mantling: Gules and argent   Motto: In coelo
quies   Winged skull in base
For Francis Hurt Sitwell, who d. 16 Aug. 1793.   (B.P. 1949 ed.)

3. Dexter background black
Sitwell, but barry of eight or and argent, impaling, Or three bars gules,
in chief a label of five points sable (Stovin), in centre chief of shield the
Badge of Ulster
Crest: A demi-lion rampant sable holding a shield per pale or and
argent   Mantling: Gules and argent   Motto: Ne cede malis
For Sir Sitwell Sitwell, 1st Bt., who m. 2nd, 1798, Sarah Caroline, dau.
of James Stovin, of Whitgift Hall, Yorks, and d. 14 July
1811.   (B.P. 1949 ed.)

4. Dexter background black
Sitwell, impaling, Qly, 1st and 4th, Argent a saltire engrailed gules, a
chief engrailed gules (Tait), 2nd and 3rd, Argent two ravens hanging
paleways sable with an arrow through both heads fessways proper
(Murdoch), at fess point of shield the Badge of Ulster
Crest and mantling: As 2.   Motto: As 3.
For Sir George Sitwell, 2nd Bt., who m. 1818, Susan, eldest dau. of
Craufurd Tait, of Clackmannan, and d. 12 Mar. 1853.   (B.P. 1949
ed.)

5. Sinister background black
Qly, 1st, Or two bars and in chief three roundels gules (Wake), 2nd and
3rd, Argent on a chief vert a cross tau between two molets pierced or
(Drury), 4th, Argent a cross between four fleurs-de-lys sable (Fenton),
over all the Badge of Ulster, impaling, Sitwell
Motto: Resurgam   Cherub's head at each top corner of shield and
winged skull in base
For Mary, dau. of Francis Sitwell, who m. Sir William Wake, 9th Bt.,
and d. 22 Nov. 1791.   (B.P. 1949 ed.)

6. Dexter background black
Sitwell, in dexter chief the Badge of Ulster   In pretence: Qly of six,
1st, Azure three molets argent within a double tressure flory counterflory
or (Murray), 2nd, Or a fess chequy argent and azure (Stewart), 3rd, Or

three pallets sable (Strabolgi), 4th, Argent on a bend azure three stags'
heads cabossed argent (Stanley), 5th, Gules three legs in armour proper,
spurred and garnished or, conjoined at the thigh in triangle (Isle of
Man), 6th, Gules two lions passant guardant argent (Strange)
Crest and mantling: As 2.   Motto: Furth fortune and fill the fetters
For Sir Sitwell Reresby Sitwell, 3rd Bt., who m. 1857, Louisa Lucy, 4th
dau. and co-heir of Col. Henry Hely-Hutchinson, of Weston Hall,
Northants, and d. 12 Apr. 1862.   (B.P. 1949 ed.)
(The hatchment painter has made an unusual and serious error in the
escutcheon of pretence, giving the arms of Murray, Earl of Dunmore,
instead of Hely-Hutchison, Earl of Dunoughmore; the motto is also that
of Murray)

TIDESWELL
1. Sinister background black
Argent a chevron azure between three roundels gules a chief azure
(Hobson), impaling, Qly, 1st and 4th, Gules a pale fusilly argent
(Statham), 2nd, Argent a griffin segreant sable beak and forelegs gules
(Meverill), 3rd, Paly embattled of eight argent and gules (Wigley)
Crest: A demi-griffin gules   Mantling: Gules and
argent   Motto: In coelo salus   Skull and crossbones in base
For Mary, dau. and co-heir of Sir John Statham, who m. 1728, Richard
Hobson, of Kirby Moorside, Yorks, and was bur. 19 Mar.
1737.   (Misc. Gen. et Her. 1901, Hobson ped.)

2. Sinister background black
Qly, 1st and 4th, Statham, 2nd and 3rd, Meverill   In pretence:
Wigley
Crest: A mailed cubit arm holding a sword proper   Mantling: Gules
and argent   Motto: Adjutor meus Deus   Skull below
For Bridget, dau. and co-heir of Henry Wigley, who m. Sir John
Statham, son of Thomas Statham, and his 1st wife, Barbara, dau and co-
heir of Cromwell Meverill, and d. 13 Dec. 1737.   (Derbys. Arch.
Soc. Journal, Vol. 4, p. 37)

3. All black background
Azure three lozenges argent in chief a crescent argent (Freeman),
impaling, Argent a cross engrailed sable between four roundels gules
(Clayton)
Crest: A demi-lion rampant gules, in its paws a lozenge
argent   Mantling: Gules and argent   Motto: Mors janua
vitae   Skull in base
For Robert Freeman, of Wheston Hall, who m. Elizabeth, dau. of Ralph
Clayton, of Gravenhough, Salop, and d. 18 Jan. 1763.   (M.I.;
Sheffield Library, Bagshaw papers)

TISSINGTON
1. Dexter background black
Qly, 1st and 4th, Gules three lions rampant or (Fitzherbert), 2nd,
Argent, in fess point a crescent gules, on a chief azure two molets or, in
centre chief a label of three points or (Clinton), 3rd, Vairy argent and
sable (Meynell)   In pretence: Or a buglehorn stringed sable
between three roses gules seeded proper (Bagshawe)
Crest: A cubit arm in armour erect the hand appearing clenched within
the gauntlet all proper   Mantling: Gules and argent   Motto:
Mors janua vitae   Skull and crossbones below
For William FitzHerbert, who m. 1709, Rachel (d. 1762), dau. and heir
of Thomas Bagshaw, of Bakewell, and d. 6 Nov. 1739.   (B.P. 1949
ed.)

2. All black background
Fitzherbert, with a crescent for difference, within the collar of the Order
of SS Michael and George, with badge pendent therefrom
Baron's coronet   Crest: As 1.   Motto: Intaminatis
honorabus   Mantle: Gules and ermine   Supporters: Two
unicorns ermine, armed, maned, unguled, ducally gorged and corded or
For Alleyne, Lord St Helens, who d. unm. 19 Feb. 1839.   (B.P.
1949 ed.)

TRUSLEY
1. All black background
Gules three crescents and a canton or (Coke), impaling, Argent two
squirrels sejant addorsed gules, in chief a martlet sable for difference
(Samwell)
Crest: A sun in splendour or   Mantling: Gules and
argent   Motto: Mors mihi vita   Skull and crossbones
below   Inscribed on frame: Robert Coke obit 23 Jany 1713/14
For Robert Coke, who m. 1677, Elizabeth, only dau. of Anthony
Samwell, and d. 23 Jan. 1713, aged 67.   (B.L.G. 1937 ed.)

2. Dexter background black
Coke, impaling, Argent two bars vert each charged with three cross
crosslets or (Ballidon)
Crest and mantling: As 1.   Motto: Omnes morti
obnoxii   Inscribed on frame: William Coke obit 18 Jany 1718/19
For William Coke, who m. 1693, Catherine, dau. and heir to Paul
Ballidon, of co. Derby, and d. 18 Jan. 1718, aged 39.   (B.L.G. 1937
ed.)

3. All black background
On a lozenge   Arms: As 2.
Cherub's head above and skull below
Inscribed on frame: Catherine Coke obit 23 March 1719/20
For Catherine, widow of William Coke, d. 23 Mar. 1719.   (Coke of
Trusley, J. T. Coke, 1880; inscr. on hatchment frame; B.L.G. 1937 ed.)

4. Sinister background black

Qly, 1st and 6th, Coke, with molet or in chief for difference, 2nd, Per chevron argent and gules in chief two roses gules slipped vert (Owen), 3rd, Argent a fess and in chief two molets gules (Odingsell), 4th, Argent on a saltire azure five water bougets argent (Sacheverell), 5th, Azure a fess engrailed between two chevrons engrailed ermine (Kirkby)   In pretence: Coke
Crest and mantling: As 1.   Motto: In coelo quies   Skull and crossbones below   Inscribed on frame: Frances Coke obit Dec. 1732
For Frances, 2nd dau. and co-heir of William Coke, who m. D'Ewes Coke, of Suckley, as his 1st wife, and d. Dec. 1732.   (Sources, as 3.)

5. All black background

Qly, 1st and 4th, Sable on a fess or between three eagles' heads couped argent three escallops gules, a canton vairy ermine and gules (Wilmot), 2nd and 3rd, Coke
Crest: An eagle's head couped argent murally gorged sable, holding in its beak an escallop gules   Mantling and motto: As 4.   Skull and crossbones below   Inscribed on frame: Edward Wilmot obit 1 Jany 1748
Although attributed to Edward Wilmot, of Spondon, Barrister-at-Law, who m. 1718, his cousin, Caherine Cassandra Isabella, dau. of William Coke, and d. 1 Jan. 1748, probably for the Rev. Francis Wilmot, Rector of Trusley, who d. unm. 21 Apr. 1818.   (Sources, as 3.)

6. Dexter background black

Coke, with a crescent sable on a crescent or in chief for difference, impaling, Wilmot, no canton
Crest: As 1.   Inscribed on frame: John Coke obit 14 Sept. 1841
For John Coke, of Debdale, who m. 1806, Susannah, dau. of Francis Ballidon Wilmot, and d.s.p. 14 Sept. 1841.   (Sources, as 3.)

7. All black background

On a lozenge surmounted by a skull
Qly of six, 1st and 6th, Coke, with a crescent or in chief for difference, 2nd, Per chevron or and gules in chief two roses gules slipped vert (Owen), 3rd, Argent a fess and in chief three molets of six points gules (Odingsell), 4th, Argent on a saltire azure five water bougets argent (Sacheverell), 5th, Argent a bear salient sable collared chained and muzzled or (Beresford)   In pretence: Wilmot, as 6., with a crescent or in chief for difference
Motto: Resurgam   Inscribed on frame: Susanna Coke obit 23 Jany 1848
For Susannah, widow of John Coke, d. 23 Jan. 1848.   (Sources, as 3.)

8. Dexter background black

Qly of twelve, 1st, Coke, 2nd, Owen, as 4., 3rd, Odingsell, as 4., 4th,
Sacheverell, 5th, Argent three hares playing bagpipes proper
(Fitzercald), 6th, Gules a snipe argent ducally gorged or (Snitterton),
7th, Azure a fess between two chevrons engrailed ermine (Kirkby), 8th,
Beresford, 9th, Per chevron argent and or three pheons sable (Hassall),
10th, Argent two bars azure each charged with three cross crosslets or
(Ballidon), 11th, Argent three roundels between two bendlets gules
(Heywood), 12th, Wilmot, as 5., impaling, Gules a lion rampant and a
bordure engrailed or (Talbot)
Crest: As 1.   Mantling: Gules and or   Motto: Non aliunde
pendere   Inscribed on frame: Edward Thomas Coke obit 26 Feby
1888
For Edward Thomas Coke, of Trusley and Debdale Hall, who m. 1835,
Diana, 2nd dau. of the Rev. John Talbot, of Ardfert Abbey, and d. 26
Feb. 1888.   (Sources, as 3.)

WILLINGTON
1. All black background

Azure a cross formy or a canton argent (Ward), impaling, Gules a cross
between twelve cross crosslets or (Woodhouse)
Crest: From a mural coronet gules a wolf's head or langued
gules   Mantling: Gules and argent   Motto: In coelo quies
For Benjamin Ward, who m. Elizabeth Woodhouse, and d. 27 Aug.
1790.   (M.I.; Burke's Commoners III, 64)

WINGERWORTH
1. All black background

On a lozenge   Gules three escallops argent (Keppel), impaling,
Azure a fess between three tigers' heads erased or (Hunloke)
Countess's coronet   Supporters: Two lions ducally crowned or
For Charlotte Susannah, dau. of Sir Henry Hunloke, Bt., who m. 1822,
as his 2nd wife, William Charles, 4th Earl of Albemarle, and d.s.p. 13
Oct. 1862.   (B.P. 1949 ed.)

2. All black background

Qly of eight, 1st and 8th, Hunloke, 2nd, Argent a fess between three
boars' heads couped sable (Alvey), 3rd, Gules three tyrwhitts or
(Tyrwhitt), 4th, Gules a chief or (Groval), 5th, Or two bars azure, a
chief qly France and England (Manners), 6th, Gules three water bougets
argent (De Ros), 7th, Argent a lion rampant sable (Charlton)
Crest: On a chapeau gules and ermine a cockatrice or   Motto:
Requiescat in pace
Unidentified
(These two hatchments were recorded in good condition soon after the
Survey began in 1952, but were subsequently destroyed 'because of
woodworm'!)

WIRKSWORTH
1. All black background
Qly, 1st, Sable a fess between three cinquefoils or (Hurt), 2nd, Gules a
wolf passant argent (Lowe), 3rd, Azure a hart trippant argent (Lowe),
4th, Argent a bugle born sable between three crescents sable each
charged with a bezant (Fawne), impaling, Argent on a mount vert a
cotton tree fructed proper, on a chief azure an inescutcheon argent
charged with a bee volant proper between two bezants (Arkwright)
Crest: A hart trippant proper attired or hurt in the flank with an arrow
or feathered argent   Mantling: Gules and argent   Motto: Mors
janua vitae
For Francis Edward Hurt, who m. 1802, Elizabeth, dau. of Richard
Arkwright, of Willersley, and d. 22 Mar. 1854.   (B.L.G. 1937 ed.)

2. Dexter background black
Qly, 1st, Per bend azure and or three molets of six points in bend
counterchanged (Gell), 2nd, Argent on a chevron sable three
quartrefoils or (Eyre), 3rd, Or three barnacles sable (Padley), 4th,
Azure crusilly three cinquefoils argent (Darcy)   In pretence: Qly,
1st and 4th, Argent on a cross between twelve gouttes gules a fleur-de-
lys or (Nicholas), 2nd and 3rd, Argent a cross engrailed between twelve
gouttes gules (Heath)
Crest: A greyhound statant sable collared or   Mantling: Gules and
argent   Motto: Ung dieu ung roy   Skull below
For Philip Gell, of Hopton Hall, who m. Georgiana Anne, dau. of
Nicholas Nicholas, of Boys Court, Kent, and d. 25 Jan.
1842.   (B.L.G. 1937 ed.)

WORMHILL
1. Dexter background black
Per pale or ermined sable and gules a buglehorn stringed between three
roses all counterchanged (Bagshawe), impaling, Per fess indented azure
and ermine two bars counterchanged, in chief a stag trippant or
(Ridgard)
Crest: From a cloud a cubit arm proper grasping a buglehorn or handle
sable, within the strings a rose gules   Mantling: Gules and
argent   Motto: Nescit servire virtus
For Sir William Chambers Bagshawe, who m. 1792, Helen, 2nd dau. of
Nathaniel Ridgard, of Gainsborough, and d. 29 June 1832.   (B.L.G.
1937 ed.)

2. Dexter background black
Qly, 1st, Bagshawe, 2nd, Per bend or and vert three molets of six points
in bend counterchanged (Gill), 3rd, Argent on a chevron three
cinquefoils argent (Westby), 4th, Argent a wyvern sejant gules (Drake),

impaling, Gules on a fess argent between three lions rampant or three
partridges proper (Partridge)
Crest: From a cloud a cubit arm proper grasping a buglehorn sable,
within the strings a rose gules   Mantling: Gules and
argent   Motto: Forma flos fama fatus
For William John Bagshawe, who m. 1822, Sarah, 3rd dau. of William
Partridge, of Bishop's Wood, co. Hereford, and d. 1 June
1851.   (B.L.G. 1937 ed.)

3. All white background
Or a buglehorn sable stringed vert between three roses gules barbed and
seeded proper (Bagshawe)
Crest: As 1.   Mantling: Gules and argent   Motto: Mors janua
vitae
Unidentified

LEICESTERSHIRE AND RUTLAND

by

F. M. Best

Leicester, Newarke Houses Museum: For Henry, 2nd Marquis of
Anglesea, 1869
(*Photograph by Leicester Museums and Art Gallery*)

INTRODUCTION*

Some 84 hatchments have been recorded in Leicestershire, distributed fairly evenly over the county. They generally appear in good condition and some have recently been repaired or repainted, such as those at Nevill Holt which were restored by a member of the Nevill family now living far from his ancestral home. They vary in size, a particularly large one being at Twycross, that of the 1st Earl Howe, and they are often placed high on church walls where it is difficult to decipher details, so inevitably there must be some errors in recording. All known hatchments are found in churches with the exception of two in Husbands Bosworth Old Hall, one in Quenby Hall, and one in the Newarke Houses Museum at Leicester: the latter is a Staffordshire hatchment from Beaudesert Hall, being that of the 2nd Marquess of Anglesey. At least two recorded hatchments have disappeared in recent years, of Sir Edmund Cradock-Hartopp at Knighton, and of Clement Winstanley, at Braunstone, which was destroyed by fire.

There are no very early hatchments; about twenty are 18th century, but the majority belong to the 19th century. Ashby-de-la-Zouch, which is rich in monumental heraldry of the Hastings, Earls of Huntingdon, has the largest number of hatchments in the county, namely seven. This is followed by Hungarton and Swithland with six each. Bottesford in the far north, whose chancel abounds with tombs and monuments with their interesting heraldry of the Manners, Earls and Dukes of Rutland, whose seat was at nearby Belvoir Castle, is one of three churches with five hatchments each.

There is an expected variety of style throughout the county and their accuracy also varies. There appears to be only one pair of duplicates, the Countess of Loudon's hatchment found

*This introduction includes both Leicestershire (pp. 59-81) and Rutland (pp. 83-86).

at both Ashby-de-la-Zouch and Willesley. For those who love many quarterings there are those at Market Bosworth of Sir Willoughby Wolstan Dixie where 24 quarterings impale seven more, with the punning motto 'Quod dixi dixi', and at Swinford where the Otway coat has in pretence an escutcheon of 35 quarterings which are repeated on the sinister shield. Of interest at Nevill Holt is the foreign appearance of one hatchment where the arms of Count Migliorucci impale Nevill and the whole is placed on a Maltese cross, but generally speaking the hatchments of Leicestershire reflect the easy going life of the gentry of this delectable heart-shaped county in the heart of England.

Only ten hatchments have been recorded in Rutland. Seven of these are in churches and include a fairly recent example at Morcott, for Caroline Frances Rowley, who died in 1900. The remaining three are in the Bede House at Lyddington; they are all for Cecils, Earls of Exeter. I am indebted to the late Mr. Keith Train, F.S.A., for checking these ten hatchments both for presence and accuracy of blazon.

F. M. Best,
Besley House, Bishop's Frome,
Worcester

LEICESTERSHIRE

ANSTEY

1. Dexter background black

Per saltire or and argent three martlets between two bars gules (Martin of Anstey Pastures)   In pretence: Argent a chevron engrailed between two escallops in chief and a cross formy in base gules (Richards of Normanton)

Crest: A talbot's head erased argent, eared gules, charged with three cross crosslets gules and collared vert   Mantling: Gules and argent   Motto: Sure and stedfast

For William Martin, of Anstey Pastures, who m. 1807, Ann Ward (d. 15 Apr. 1855) only child of John Richards, and d. 24 July 1850.   (B.L.G. 18th ed.)

ASHBY-DE-LA-ZOUCH

1. All black background

On a lozenge   Qly, 1st, Argent a maunch sable (Hastings), 2nd, France and England qly, a label of three points argent (Plantagenet), 3rd, Per pale or and sable a saltire engrailed counterchanged (Pole), 4th, Sable two bars and in chief three roundels argent (Hungerford)   In pretence: Qly, 1st and 4th, Or three pales sable a canton ermine (Shirley), 2nd and 3rd, France and England qly, a bordure argent (Plantagenet)

Countess's coronet   Motto: In veritate victoria   Supporters: Dexter, A man tiger rampant guardant or   Sinister, A talbot ermine ducally gorged or   Mantle: Gules and ermine

For Selina, dau. and co-heiress of Washington, 2nd Earl Ferrers, who m. 1728, Theophilus, 9th Earl of Huntingdon, and d. 17 June 1791.   (B.P. 1949 ed.)

2. All black background

Qly, 1st, Hastings, 2nd, Plantagenet, but no label, 3rd, Pole, 4th, Hungerford

Earl's coronet   Crest: A bull's head erased sable, ducally gorged and armed or   Mantle and motto: As 1.   Supporters: Two man tigers rampant guardant or

For Francis, 10th Earl of Huntingdon, who d.s.p. 2 Oct. 1789.   (B.P. 1949 ed.)

3. All black background (should be dexter black)

Qly of twelve, 1st, Argent a fess between three pheons sable (Rawdon), 2nd, Hastings, 3rd, Hungerford, 4th, Argent three toads sable

59

(Botreaux), 5th, Or three roundels gules a label of three points azure
(Courtenay), 6th, Paly wavy of six or and gules (Moleyns), 7th, Pole,
8th, Plantagenet as 1., 9th, Gules a saltire argent a label of three points
compony argent and azure (Nevill), 10th, Argent three lozenges
conjoined in fess gules (Montagu), 11th, England within a bordure
argent (Plantagenet), 12th, Or an eagle displayed vert
(Monthermer)   In pretence, ensigned with a countess's coronet:
Gyronny of eight gules and ermine (Campbell)
Marquess's coronet   Crests: Dexter, as 2.   Sinister, A pheon
sable and issuant therefrom a laurel branch proper   Motto:
Laboravi quiesco   Supporters: Two bears argent, muzzled and
chained or, each holding a ragged staff argent   Collar of Order of
Garter shows below shield
For Francis, 1st Marquess of Hastings, K.G., who m. 1804, Flora Muir,
Countess of Loudoun, and d. 28 Nov. 1826.   (B.P. 1949 ed.)

4. All black background

On a lozenge   Qly, 1st, Rawdon, 2nd, Hastings, 3rd, Pole, 4th,
Plantagenet as 1.   In pretence, and impaling, Campbell
Above the lozenge, to the dexter the coronet of a marchioness, and to the
sinister the coronet of a countess   Motto: I byde my
tyme   Supporters: Dexter, as 3.   Sinister, A lady nobly dressed,
plumed on the head with three feathers argent and holding in the left
hand a letter of challenge
For Flora Muir, Countess of Loudoun, widow of Francis, 1st Marquess
of Hastings. She d. 8 Jan. 1840.   (B.P. 1949 ed.)

5. Dexter background black

Qly, 1st and 4th, qly i. & iv. Hastings, ii. & iii. Rawdon, 2nd and 3rd,
Gyronny of eight ermine and gules (Campbell)   In pretence,
ensigned with a baroness's coronet: Qly, 1st and 4th, Argent three lions
rampant and a chief gules (Yelverton), 2nd and 3rd, Barry of six argent
and azure in chief three roundels gules (Grey de Ruthyn)
Marquess's coronet   Three crests: Dexter, A bull's head erased
sable ducally gorged or (Hastings)   Centre, A double-headed eagle
displayed gules issuant out of water proper, above and to the dexter the
sun in splendour or (Campbell)   Sinister, Out of a mural coronet
argent a pheon sable issuant therefrom a laurel branch proper
(Rawdon)   Motto: Trust winneth troth   Supporters: Two bears
argent muzzled gules and chained or each holding a ragged staff
proper   The hatchment has a gutty border counterchanged
For George Augustus, 2nd Marquess of Hastings, who m. 1831, Barbara,
Baroness Grey de Ruthyn, and d. 13 Jan. 1844.   (B.P. 1949 ed.)

6. Identical to 5., but slightly smaller

7. Sinister background black

Two shields   Dexter, Qly, 1st, qly i. & iv. Argent a maunch within a bordure engrailed sable (Hastings), ii. & iii. Or on a chief gules a demi-lion rampant argent (Abney), 2nd, Sable on a bend argent three molets gules (Clifton), 3rd, Azure a cross moline or (Molyneux), 4th, Gules crusilly or three lucies hauriant two and one argent
(Lucy)   In pretence, ensigned with a countess's coronet: Qly of six, 1st, qly i. & iv. Hastings, with bordure, ii. & iii. Abney, 2nd, Hastings as 1., 3rd, Rawdon, 4th, Barry of six sable and argent in chief three roundels argent (Hungerford), 5th, Plantagenet with label, 6th, Campbell as 5.   Sinister, as escutcheon of pretence on dexter shield ensigned with a countess's coronet   Supporters: Dexter, A knight in armour holding a spear in his right hand proper and plumed on the head with three feathers gules   Sinister, as sinister of 4.   Motto (below and between both shields) Deus meus illumina tenebras meas
For Edith Maud, Countess of Loudoun, who m. 1853, Charles Frederick Clifton (both asumming by Act of Parliament in 1859 the name and arms of Abney-Hastings only), and d. 23 Jan. 1874.   (B.P. 1949 ed.)
(There is an identical hatchment in the parish church at Willesley)

ASHBY FOLVILLE

1. All black background

Qly, 1st and 4th, Sable on a bend argent three lozenges sable (Carington), 2nd and 3rd, Argent a cross gules between four peacocks azure (Smith)
Crests: Dexter, Out of a ducal coronet or a unicorn's head sable, armed and crined argent   Sinister, A peacock's head erased proper ducally gorged or   Mantling: Gules and argent   Motto: Fides semper firma   A very small hatchment painted on wood, *c.* 18 in. by 18 in.   Unframed
Probably for Richard Smith-Carington, who d. at Ashby Folville, 9 Feb. 1901.   (B.L.G. 1937 ed.)
(The early history of this small hatchment is unknown; it was found only recently in an antique shop in Brighton, but it almost certainly came originally from Ashby Folville)

BARKBY

1. Sinister background black

Or a chevron gules between three horseshoes sable (Pochin), impaling, Vert three stags trippant a bordure argent (Trollope)
Motto: Memoria pia aeterna
For Mary, only dau. of Thomas Trollope, of Bourne, Lincs, who m. as his 2nd wife, Thomas Pochin, High Sheriff 1711, and d. 7 May 1732, aged 31. He d. 30 Aug. 1751.   (M.I.)

2. All black background

Pochin arms only
Crest: A harpy, winged, full-faced and tail twisted round leg proper   Mantling: Gules and argent   Motto: Mors janua vita

For William Pochin, eldest son of Thomas Pochin, and his 2nd wife, Mary Trollope. He d. 10 Sep. 1798, aged 67.   (B.L.G. 2nd ed.; M.I.)

3. Dexter background black

Pochin, impaling, Argent on a bend gules three stags' heads cabossed or (Norman)

Crest: A harpy or   Mantling: Gules and argent   Motto: Mors janua vitae

For George Pochin, High Sheriff 1828, who m. 1811, Elizabeth (d. 3 Dec. 1861), 2nd dau. of Richard Norman, of Melton Mowbray, and d. 29 Dec. 1831.   (B.L.G. 1937 ed.)

BOTTESFORD

1. Dexter background black

Or two bars azure a chief qly azure and gules in the first and fourth qrs two fleur-de-lys and in the second and third qrs a lion passant guardant or (Manners), impaling, Qly, 1st and 4th, Argent a fret sable (Tollemache), 2nd and 3rd, Azure an imperial crown proper between three molets or within a double tressure flory counterflory or (Murray)

Crest: On a chapeau gules and ermine a peacock in its pride proper   Mantling: Gules and argent   Motto: Pour y parvenir

For John Manners, of Hanby Hall, Lincs, and Buckminster, Leics, who m. 1765, Lady Louisa Tollemache, afterwards in her own right Countess of Dysart, and d. 23 Sept. 1792. She d. 22 Sept. 1840.   (B.P. 1949 ed.)

(There is another hatchment for John Manners at Grantham, Lincs)

2. All black background

Two shields   Dexter, within the Garter, Manners   Sinister, Argent a canton sable (Sutton)

Duke's coronet   Crest: As 1.   Mantle: Gules and ermine   Motto: As 1.   Supporters: Two unicorns argent

For John, 3rd Duke of Rutland, K.G., who m. 1717, Bridget (d. 16 June 1734), dau. and sole heiress of Robert, 2nd Baron Lexington, and d. 29 May 1779.   (B.P. 1949 ed.)

3. All black background

Within the Garter, Manners, impaling, Qly France and England within a bordure compony argent and azure (Somerset)

Duke's coronet   Crest, mantle and motto: As 2.   Supporters: Dexter, A unicorn argent   Sinister, A panther guardant argent semy of roundels gules, collared and chained or

For Charles, 4th Duke of Rutland, K.G., who m. 1775, Mary Isabella (d. 2 Sept. 1831), youngest dau. of Charles, 4th Duke of Beaufort, and d. 24 Oct. 1787.   (B.P. 1949 ed.)

4. Sinister background black
Two shields   Dexter, within the Garter, Manners   Sinister,
Manners, impaling, Gules on a bend between six cross crosslets fitchy
argent the Augmentation of Flodden (Howard)
Duchess's coronet   Mantle and motto: As 2.   Supporters: Two
unicorns argent, armed and maned or
For Elizabeth, dau. of Frederick, 5th Earl of Carlisle, K.G., who m.
1799, John Henry, 5th Duke of Rutland, K.G., and d. 29 Nov. 1825. He
d. 20 Jan. 1857.   (B.P. 1949 ed.)

5. All black background
Manners arms only, with a crescent azure for difference
Crest and motto: As 1.   Supporters: As 4.   Winged skull below
Probably for Thomas Baptist Manners, 2nd son of John, 1st Duke of
Rutland, who d. unm. 29 June 1705, and was buried at
Bottesford   (Nichols' Leics, Vol. 2, p. 67)

BRAUNSTONE
1. All black background
Qly, 1st, Or two bars azure in chief three crosses formy gules
(Winstanley), 2nd, Argent on a bend engrailed sable three fleurs-de-lys
argent (Holt), 3rd, Argent a chevron gules a label of three points gules
(Prideaux), 4th, Argent two chevrons engrailed gules on a canton gules
a mascle or (Reynardson), impaling, Argent an eagle displayed sable,
on a quarter or a fess dancetty between seven billets ermine (Parkyns)
Crest: A cockatrice displayed or, crested and jelloped
gules   Mantling: Gules and argent   Motto: In coelo quies
For Clement Winstanley, High Sheriff 1774, who m. 1774, Jane, eldest
dau. of Sir Thomas Parkyns, 3rd Bt., and d. 17 May 1808. She d. 8 Jan.
1807.   (B.L.G. 1937 ed.; Nichols, Leicestershire, Vol. IV)
(This hatchment recorded in 1956, has since been destroyed in a fire)

2. All black background
Qly, as 1., but mascle argent and no impalement
Crest and mantling: As 1.   Motto: Resurgam
Probably for Clement Winstanley, High Sheriff 1815, who d. unm. 1855,
or for his nephew, James Beaumont Winstanley, who d. unm. 7 July
1862.   (B.L.G. 1937 ed.)

CADEBY
1. Dexter background black
Azure a lion rampant and a chief or, in centre chief the Badge of Ulster

(Dixie), impaling, Azure a griffin segreant argent a bordure engrailed
ermine (Walters)
Crest: An ounce sejant proper ducally gorged or   Mantling: Azure
and or   Motto: Quod dixi dixi
For Sir Alexander Beaumont Dixie, 10th Bt., who m. 1843, Maria
Catharine, youngest dau. of the Rev. Charles Walters, Rector of
Bramdean, Hants, and d. 8 Jan. 1872. She d. 16 Apr. 1902.   (B.P.
1949 ed.)

EASTWELL
1. Dexter background black
Argent on a chevron sable three quatrefoils or (Eyre), impaling, Qly
argent and gules a bend sable (Widdrington)
Crest: A leg erect in armour couped at the thigh proper, kneecap and
spur or   Mantling: Gules and argent   Motto: Omnis spiritus
laudet Dominum
For Rowland Eyre, who m. Mary, dau. of William, 4th Baron
Widdrington, and d.   (B.E.P.)

EDMONDTHORPE
1. Dexter background black
Argent a chevron gules between three horseshoes sable (Pochin),
impaling, Or two bars azure in chief three crosses formy gules
(Winstanley)
Crest: A harpy proper   Mantling: Gules and argent   Motto:
Resurgam
For Charles William Pochin, of Barkby, who m. Anne Jane, dau. of
Clement Winstanley, of Braunstone, and d. 17 June 1817, aged
40.   (B.L.G. 2nd ed.; M.I.)

ENDERBY
1. All black background
Argent on a bend sable a hawk's lure argent (Brook), impaling, Gules
on a chief indented argent three annulets azure, a martlet or for cadency
(Hirst)
Crest: A goat's head erased or   No helm or mantling   Motto:
En Dieu ma foi
Probably for Charles Brook, J.P. of Enderby Hall, who d. *c.* 1870-
76.   (White's Directory of Leicestershire, 1877)
(Perhaps also used for his widow, as it seems that the sinister black
background was painted later than the dexter)

GROBY
1. Dexter background black
Qly, 1st and 4th, Barry of six argent and azure (Grey), 2nd and 3rd,
Argent three boars' heads couped and erect sable (Booth)

Earl's coronet   Crest: A unicorn passant ermine, armed, maned, tufted and unguled or in front of a sun in splendour   Motto: A ma puissance   Supporters: Two unicorns as in the crest
Probably for George Harry, 5th Earl of Stamford, son of Harry, 4th Earl of Stamford, and Lady Mary Booth, only dau. and heiress of George, last Earl of Warrington. He d. 28 May 1819.   (B.P. 1949 ed.)
(There are further hatchments for the 5th Earl at Bowdon, Cheshire and Enville, Staffs.)

HALLATON
1. Dexter background black
Azure a fess between three estoiles or (Thwaites), impaling, Sable six lozenges conjoined in fess argent in chief three escallops or (Dent)
Crest: (on an open, affronté helm) A cock, wings elevated argent, combed and wattled gules   Mantling: Gules and argent   Motto: Dum spiro spero
Unidentified

HUNGARTON
1. All black background
On a lozenge   Argent two bars and in chief a lion passant guardant gules (Burnaby), impaling, Argent a cross sable between four choughs proper (Edwyn)
Motto: Resurgam
For Anna, dau. and heir of John Edwyn of Baggrave Hall, who m. the Ven. Andrew Burnaby, D.D., and d. 16 Mar. 1812. He d. 9 Mar. 1812.   (B.L.G. 18th ed.)

2. Dexter background black
Qly, 1st and 4th, Burnaby, 2nd and 3rd, Edwyn   In pretence: Argent a fess between three mallets sable (Browne)
Crest: A demi-man sable in the dexter hand a bunch of columbine flowers and round the neck a rope proper   Mantling: Gules and argent   Motto: Mors janua vitae   Skull in base
For Edwyn Andrew Burnaby, D.L., J.P., of Baggrave Hall, who m. 1796, Mary (d. 11 Jan. 1858), dau. and heiress of the Rev. William Browne, Rector of Burrow, and d. 1 Oct. 1825.   (B.L.G. 18th ed.)

3. Dexter background black
Azure a chevron ermine between three leopards' faces or (Ashby)   In pretence: Argent a chevron between three hinds trippant gules (Hinde)
Crest: Out of a mural coronet argent a leopard's face or   Mantling: Gules and argent   Motto: Mors janua vitae   Winged skull below

For Shuckbrugh Ashby, High Sheriff 1758, who m. Elizabeth, dau. and sole heiress of Richard Hinde, of Cold Ashby, co. Northampton, and d. 27 Jan. 1792. She d. 8 Nov. 1795.   (B.L.G. 2nd ed.; M.I.)

4. Dexter background black
Or on a chief indented azure three roundels argent a crescent gules for difference (Latham)   In pretence: Ashby
Crest: On a chapeau gules and or a pelican vulning itself argent   Mantling: Gules and argent   Motto: Spes mea in Christo   Skull in base
For William Latham, who m. 1770, Mary Elizabeth, dau. and co-heir of Shuckbrugh Ashby, and d. 7 Mar. 1807.   (B.L.G. 2nd ed.; G.M.)

5. All black background
On a lozenge   Arms: As 4.   Skull in base
For Mary Elizabeth, widow of William Latham. She d. 26 July 1815.   (B.L.G. 2nd ed.; G.M.)

6. Sinister background black
Argent three spearheads sable tipped or in centre chief the Badge of Ulster (Apreece)   In pretence: Ashby
Motto: Resurgam
For Dorothea, dau. and co-heir of Shuckbrugh Ashby, who m. Sir Thomas Hussey Apreece, Bt., and d. 26 Dec. 1822.   (B.L.G. 2nd ed.; M.I.)

HUSBANDS BOSWORTH Old Hall
1. Dexter background black
Azure a bend engrailed argent cotised or (Fortescue)   In pretence, and impaling, Or a lion passant sable armed and langued gules in chief three piles in point sable (Login)
Crest: A tyger passant argent   Mantling: Gules and argent   Motto: In coelo quies
For Charles Fortescue, of Husbands Bosworth, who m. Elizabeth Login, of Idbury, Oxon, and d. 1732.   (Burke's Commoners, II, 647)

2. All black background
Gules three chevronels vair (Turvile), impaling, Azure three molets of six points or, on a chief argent a demi-lion issuant gules (Van der Lancken)
Crest: A dove, in its beak an olive branch proper   Mantling: Gules and argent   Motto: Mors janua vitae   Skull in base
For George Fortescue Turvile, of Husbands Bosworth, who m. 1826, Henrietta, dau. of Baron Adolph Van der Lancken, of Galenbeck in the Duchy of Mecklenberg Schwerin, and d. 10 Dec. 1859.   (B.L.G. 5th ed.)

KIRKBY MALLORY
1. Sinister background black
Qly, 1st and 4th, Or fretty gules a canton ermine (Noel), Sable a chevron between three leopards' faces or (Wentworth), 3rd, Gules on a chief indented sable three martlets or (Lovelace)   In pretence: Sable on a fess or between three cinquefoils argent two molets sable (Lamb) Baroness's coronet   Motto: Penses a bien   Supporters: Two griffins argent collared or   Skull and crossbones below
For Judith, dau. and co-heir of William Lamb, of Wellsborough, Leics, who m. Edward, 9th Baron Wentworth, and d. 3 Dec. 1761.   (B.P. 1875 ed.)

2. All black background
Qly, as 1.   In pretence: Qly, 1st and 4th, Azure a lion rampant argent within a bordure argent charged with eight roundels gules (Henley), 2nd and 3rd, Argent three battering rams fesswise in pale proper (Bertie)
Viscount's coronet   Motto and supporters: As 1.
For Thomas, 2nd Viscount Wentworth, who m. 1788, Mary, dau. of Robert, 1st Earl of Northington, and d. 17 Apr. 1815. She d. 29 June 1814.   (B.P. 1949 ed.)

KNIGHTON
1. All black background
Qly, 1st and 4th, Sable a chevron between three otters passant argent (Hartopp), 2nd and 3rd, Per saltire gules and argent crusilly and three boars' heads couped all counterchanged (Cradock), over all the Badge of Ulster, impaling, Gules on a chevron between three garbs argent three escallops sable (Eden)
Crests: A pelican proper   2. A mailed hand holding a sword piercing a boar's head proper   Motto: Resurgam
For Sir Edmund Cradock-Hartopp, 2nd Bt., who m. 1824, Mary Jane Eden, dau. of Morton, 1st Baron Henley, and d. 3 Apr. 1849.   (B.P. 1949 ed.)
(This hatchment was recorded in 1956, but has since disappeared)

LEICESTER, Newarke Houses Museum
1. ¾ background black, i.e. background of arms of 3rd wife left white
Sable on a cross engrailed between four eagles displayed argent five lions passant sable (Paget), impaling three coats, per fess and in chief per pale (1) Gyronny of eight sable and or (Campbell), (2) Ermine two chevrons azure (Bagot), (3) Per pale or and gules from a cloud issuant from the sinister an arm extended in armour proper grasping a sword argent, out of the base three spikes of a lily plant flowered argent slipped vert (Burnand)
Marquess's coronet   Crest: A demi-heraldic tiger sable, maned, tufted and ducally gorged or   Mantling: Gules and

ermine   Motto: Per il suo contrario   Supporters: Two heraldic
tigers as in the crest
For Henry, 2nd Marquess of Anglesey, who m. 1st, 1819, Eleanora (d. 3
July 1828), dau. of Col. John Campbell of Shawfield; 2nd, 1833,
Henrietta Maria (d. 22 Mar. 1844), 3rd dau. of the Rt. Hon. Sir Charles
Bagot; 3rd, 1860, Ellen Jane (d. 2 June 1874), dau. of George Burnand,
and d. 7 Feb. 1869.   (B.P. 1949 ed.)

LOCKINGTON
1. Dexter background black
Qly, 1st and 4th, Argent a chevron embattled between three battleaxes
sable (Bainbridge), 2nd, Azure a gauntlet or (Lacock), 3rd, Or a bend
cotised sable (Harley)
Crest: A goat statant sable   Mantling: Gules and
argent   Motto: Verus honor honesta
Probably for Philip Henry Bainbrigge, son of William Bainbrigge and
Mary, dau. and co-heir of Philip Laycock of Woodborough, Notts; he m.
Katherine, dau. of Thomas Allicock of Lambley, and d.s.p. 27 July
1769, aged 49.   (M.I.)

2. Dexter background black
Qly, 1st, Per fess indented argent and sable three falcons
counterchanged (Story), 2nd and 3rd, Gules a gauntlet or (for Lacock),
4th, Argent a chevron embattled counter-embattled between three
battleaxes sable (Bainbrigge), impaling, Per chevron azure and or in
chief two falcons rising or (Stevens)
Crests: Dexter, A falcon proper   Sinister, A cock gules holding a
gauntlet or   Mantling: Gules and argent   Motto: In coelo quies
For the Rev. Philip Story, Vicar of Lockington, who m. Martha, dau. of
the Rev. Richard Stevens, Rector of Bottesford, and d.
(B.L.G. 5th ed.; Nichols, History of Leics, Vol. III)

LODDINGTON
1. Dexter background black
Qly, 1st and 4th, Sable a lion passant argent between three scaling
ladders or (Morris), 2nd, Gules on a chief argent two molets gules
(   ), 3rd, Argent a fess gules between three cross crosslets fitchy
sable (   )
Crest: On a mount vert a tower or   Mantling: Gules and
argent   Motto: Mors janua vitae
Probably for Charles Campbell Morris, of Loddington Mill, who d. 5
June 1850, aged 50.   (E. window erected to him by his widow,
Mary, in 1857)

LUBENHAM
1. Dexter background black
Gules a fess humetty or between three trestles argent (Stratford)   In

pretence: Qly, 1st and 4th, Or five ermine spots between two barrulets sable, all between two lions passant sable (   ), 2nd and 3rd, Azure a chevron engrailed between three crescents argent (Palmer)
Crest: An arm embowed in armour proper garnished or, holding in the hand a scimitar proper, hilted or   Mantling: Gules and argent   Motto: Resurgam
For F. P. Stratford, of Thorpe Lubenham Hall, who d. 1841.   (V.C.H.)

MARKET BOSWORTH
1. Dexter background black
Qly of twenty-four, 1st, Azure a lion rampant and a chief or (Dixie), 2nd, Argent a saltire engrailed between four escallops sable (Beridge), 3rd, Argent on a saltire gules nine cross crosslets or (Crathorne), 4th, Sable a chevron between three molets argent (Shuckbrugh), 5th, Sable a bend between six estoiles or (   ), 6th, Argent, on a saltire engrailed gules a molet or (   ), 7th, Gules seven mascles conjoined three, three and one or (Quincy), 8th, Gules a cinquefoil ermine (Earl of Leicester), 9th, Gules a pale or (Grantesmainell), 10th, Azure a lion rampant argent armed or (Alan, Lord of Galloway), 11th, Argent an inescutcheon within a tressure gules (David, Earl of Huntingdon), 12th, Gules a saltire argent (Neville), 13th, Azure a wolf's head erased argent (Hugh Lupus, Earl of Chester), 14th, Gules a lion rampant vair (Everingham), 15th, Azure a fess between three cinquefoils or (Maureward), 16th, Argent a maunch sable (Hastings), 17th, Or on two bars gules three water bougets two and one argent (Willoughby), 18th, Vert three stags trippant or (Green), 19th, Barry of six gules and argent (Pusey), 20th, Argent a chevron engrailed between three trefoils slipped sable (Clay), 21st, Sable a saltire between four cross crosslets or (   ), 22nd, Ermine on a fess gules three annulets or (   ), 23rd, Paly of six argent and azure (Strelley), 24th, Argent a molet pierced sable (Ashton), the Badge of Ulster, impaling, Qly, 1st and 4th, qly i. & iv. Gules a lion rampant reguardant or (Lloyd), ii. & iii. Argent three boars' heads couped gules (Elyston Glodrudd), 2nd, Gules a fess between six cross crosslets fitchy or (   ), 3rd, Sable a doubleheaded eagle displayed argent (   )
Crest: An ounce sejant proper ducally gorged or   Mantling: Azure and argent   Mottoes: Quod dixi dixi   Resurgam
For Sir Willoughby Wolstan Dixie, 8th Bt., who m. 1841, Louisa Anne, dau. of Lt.-Gen. Sir Evan Lloyd, K.C.H., of Ferney Hall, Salop, and d. 23 July 1850. She d. 25 Jan. 1864.   (B.P. 1949 ed.)

MELTON MOWBRAY
1. Dexter background black
Or a chevron cotised between three demi-griffins the two in chief respectant sable (Smith), impaling, Argent on a fess sable three molets or (Lyster)

Crest: An elephant's head or, tusked argent   Mantling: Gules and
argent   Motto: Mors janua vitae
For Thomas Smith, of Keyworth, who m. Dorothy, dau. of John Lyster,
of Sysonby, and d.   (B.L.G. 2nd ed.)

2. Dexter background black

Argent on a bend gules three stags' heads cabossed or, a crescent or for
difference (Norman), impaling, Or two bars azure a chief qly azure and
gules in the first and fourth qrs two fleurs-de-lys and in the second and
third qrs a lion passant guardant or (Manners)
Crest: A stoper   Mantling: Gules and argent   Motto: Resurgam
Probably for Richard Norman, who m. 1798, Elizabeth Isabella (d. 5
Oct. 1853), dau. of Charles, 4th Duke of Rutland, K.G., and d.
1847.   (B.P. 1949 ed.; B.L.G. 5th ed.)
(There were at least two other Norman/Manners marriages)

3. All black background

Azure a chevron ermine between three talbots (should be otters) argent
(Hartopp), impaling, Argent on a chevron between three maunches
azure three annulets or (Mansfield)
Crest: Out of a ducal coronet or a pelican argent vulning herself
proper   Mantling: Gules and argent
For Chiverton Hartopp, of Welby, who m. Catherine, dau. of Thomas
Mansfield, of West Leeke, and d. 2 Apr. 1759, aged 68. She d. 8 Aug.
1755, aged 54.   (Burke's Commoners; M.I. in church)

NEVILL HOLT

1. All black background

On a lozenge surmounted by the coronet of a countess   Dexter, two
coats per pale   1. Gules the dexter half of an eagle dislayed
crowned and legged or 2. Or a lion rampant sable debruised by a fess
embattled counterembattled gules, on a chief azure three fleurs-de-lys or
(Migliorucci), impaling, Gules a saltire ermine (Nevill)   Lozenge
placed on a Maltese cross and a Maltese cross hangs beneath
Crest: A dove rising argent armed and beaked gules holding in the beak
an ear of corn or   Mantling: Gules and argent   Motto: Dieu
mihi providebit
For Mary, dau. and co-heiress of Henry Nevill, who m. Cosmas, Count
Migliorucci, and d. 1742.   (B.L.G. 5th ed.)

2. Dexter background black

Qly, 1st and 4th, Gules a saltire ermine (Nevill), 2nd and 3rd, Argent
fretty gules on a canton argent a galley sable (Nevill), impaling, Sable
a chevron between three spades argent (Gardiner)
Crest: A bull's head ermine ducally gorged or   Mantling: Gules
and argent   Motto: Ne vile velis

For Cosmas Nevill, who m. 1788, Maria Annabella, dau. of William
Gardiner, and d. 1 June 1829.   (B.L.G. 18th ed.; M.I.)

3. All black background
. Gules a saltire ermine (Nevill), impaling, Azure two bendlets between
six crosses formy or (Bingham)
Crest: Out of a ducal coronet or a bull's head ermine armed
or   Mantling and motto: As 2.
For Charles Nevill, who m. 1822, Lady Georgiana Bingham, dau. of
Richard, 3rd Earl of Lucan, and d. 18 Oct. 1848, aged 57. She d. 13
July 1849, aged 50.   (B.L.G. 5th ed.; M.I.)
(In view of the background it seems probable that the hatchment was
also used for his widow)

4. All black background
Qly, 1st and 4th, Gules a saltire ermine (Nevill), 2nd and 3rd, Argent
fretty gules on a canton per pale or and argent a galley sable
(Nevill)   In pretence: Argent a saltire engrailed between four
cinquefoils gules (Napier)
Crest: Out of a ducal coronet or a bull's head erased
ermine   Mantling: Gules and argent   Motto: Mors janua vitae
Unidentified

5. All black background
Arms: Qly, as 4. only
Crest: A bull's head argent ducally gorged or   Mantling: Gules and
argent   Motto: Mors janua vitae
Probably for George Henry Nevill, elder brother of No. 2., who d.
1767.   (Nichols)

ORTON-ON-THE-HILL
1. Dexter background black
Sable an eagle displayed argent, on a canton argent a fess dancetty
sable (Perkins), impaling, Paly of six or and azure a canton ermine
(Shirley)
Crest: From a ducal coronet or a unicorn's head argent (tinctures
uncertain)   Mantling: Gules and argent   Motto: In coelo quies
For Samuel Steele Perkins, who m. Mary, dau. of Joseph Shirley, of
Burton-upon-Trent, and d. 9 May 1808. She d. 24 June
1810.   (B.L.G. 5th ed.; M.I.)

2. All brown background
Qly, 1st, Perkins, 2nd, Argent a lion rampant between three billets
azure (Steele), 3rd, Argent two bars gules on a canton gules a maunch
argent (Beardsley), 4th, Sable a chevron between three lamps argent
flammant proper (Farmer)   In pretence: Shirley

Crest: From a ducal coronet argent a unicorn's head ermine armed and maned sable   Mantling: Gules and argent   Motto: Toujours loyal   A very small hatchment, *c.* 2 ft. by 2 ft.

For Samuel Steele Perkins, d. 9 May 1808, and perhaps also used for his widow, d. 24 June 1810.   (Sources, as 1.)

PRESTWOLD

1. Dexter background black

Qly sable and or in the first quarter a cinquefoil argent with an ermine spot on each leaf (Packe), impaling, Qly, 1st and 4th, Argent a cross moline gules charged in the centre with a Garter King of Arms coronet or and in the first quarter with a roundel gules (Dugdale), 2nd and 3rd, Barry of ten argent and azure over all a lion rampant gules (Stratford) Helm in profile with visor open showing a man's face   Crest: A lion's head erased or collared sable, on the collar three cinquefoils ermine   Mantling: Gules and argent   Motto: In coelo quies

For Charles James Packe, of Prestwold Hall, who m. 1791, Penelope (d. 17 June 1841), eldest dau. of Richard Geast Dugdale, of Blyth Hall, co. Warwick, and d. 1 Mar. 1837.   (B.L.G. 1937 ed.)

QUENBY Hall

1. All black background

Qly, 1st and 4th, Argent a canton sable (Sutton), 2nd and 3rd, Argent a cross flory azure (Lexington), over all the Badge of Ulster, impaling, Azure a cross engrailed or between four roses argent (Burton)

Crest: A wolf's head erased gules   Mantling: Gules and argent   Motto: Tout jours prest

For Sir Richard Sutton, 2nd Bt., who m. 1810, Mary Elizabeth, dau. of Benjamin Burton, and d. 13 Nov. 1855.   (B.P. 1949 ed.)

ROTHLEY Temple Chapel

1. Dexter background black

Argent ten roundels four, three, two and one gules, in chief a label of three points azure (Babington), impaling, Azure a chevron argent between three linnets proper (Cardale)

Crest: A dragon's head between two wings gules   Motto: Mors janua vitae

For Thomas Babington, of Rothley Temple, who m. 1758, Lydia, dau. of the Rev. Joseph Cardale, Vicar of Hinckley, and d. 20 June 1776. She d. 4 May 1791.   (B.L.G. 7th ed.; M.I.)

2. Dexter background black

Babington, impaling, Gules two arrows heads downwards in saltire argent surmounted by a fess chequy argent and gules between three buckles within a bordure indented or (Macaulay)

Crest: As 1.   Mantling: Gules and argent   Motto: Resurgam

For Thomas Babington, of Rothley Temple, who m. 1787, Jean, dau. of the Rev. John Macauley, A.M., Minister of Cardross, and d. 21 Nov. 1837.   (B.L.G. 7th ed.)

3. Dexter background black

Or on each of three escutcheons sable a pheon argent (Parker), impaling, Babington
Crest: An arm, holding a spear proper   Mantling: Gules and argent   Motto: Caveo
For Vice-Chancellor Sir James Parker, A.M., Barrister-at-Law, who m. Mary, dau. of Thomas Babington, and d. 1852. She d. 20 July 1858.   (B.L.G. 7th ed.)

SCRAPTOFT

1. All black background

On a lozenge   Paly of sixteen embattled argent and gules (Wigley)
For Ann, youngest and last surviving dau. of Sir Edward Wigley. She d. 16 Apr. 1786.   (M.I.)

2. Dexter background black

Qly, 1st and 4th, Sable a chevron in the dexter chief a cross crosslet argent, in the first quarter a crescent argent for difference (Pares), 2nd and 3rd, Azure on a pale engrailed or a lion rampant gules, in chief two molets and in base two crescents argent (Lightbody), impaling, Qly of six, 1st, Argent two bars and in chief a lion passant guardant gules (Burnaby), 2nd, Argent a cross sable between four choughs proper (Aylmer), 3rd, Argent a fess between three martels sable (Browne), 4th, Argent a chevron between three roundels gules (Sherard), 5th, Or fretty gules a canton ermine (Noel), 6th, Burnaby
Crest: A demi-griffin or   Mantling: Gules and argent   Motto: Pares cum paribus
For John Tylston Pares, who m. Mary, dau. of Edwyn Andrew Burnaby of Baggrave Hall, Leics, and d. 23 Nov. 1831, aged 35. She d. 1858.   (Burke's Commoners, III, 606; M.I.)

SHEPSHED

1. Sinister background black

Two shields   Dexter, within the Order of the Bath, Azure a tilting spear in fess argent the point to the dexter between three boars' heads or (Gordon)   Sinister, within a circlet or, Gordon, impaling, Azure three doves rising argent (Alsop)
Supporters: Two greyhounds argent, collared azure rimmed or dependent therefrom a shield gules   Motto: Virtute non astutia   Skull in base
For Mary, dau. of Thomas Alsop, widow of Samuel Phillipps, of Garendon Park, who m. Sir William Gordon, K.B., and d. 5 Aug. 1796, aged 59. He d. 26 Jan. 1798.   (B.L.G. 2nd ed.)

2. Dexter background black
Qly, 1st and 4th, Azure a chevron argent cotised or between three
falcons close argent (Phillips), 2nd and 3rd, Qly gules and azure a cross
or ermined sable between four lions' heads couped argent each charged
with a cross crosslet fitchy sable (March), impaling, Or on a chief azure
three lions rampant or (Lisle)
Crest: A demi-griffin sable, winged, collared and chained or, holding a
shield, Azure a lion rampant or   Mantling: Gules and argent
For Thomas March Phillipps, who m. 1777, Susan, dau. of Charles
Lisle, of Wodyton and Moyles Court, and d. Mar. 1817. She d. 5 Dec.
1838.   (B.L.G. 18th ed.)

3. All black background
Qly, 1st and 4th, Azure a chevron between three falcons close argent
(Phillipps), 2nd, Qly gules and azure a cross moline ermine between
four lions' heads erased or (March), 3rd, Lisle, impaling, Argent three
lozenges gules (Ducarel)
Three crests   Dexter, A demi-griffin or, holding a shield, Azure a
lion rampant or   Centre, A demi-lion or holding a cross moline
gules   Sinister, A stag trippant proper   Mantling: Azure and
argent   Motto: Quod justum non quod utile   Supporters: Two
stags proper
For Charles March Phillipps, son of Thomas and Susan, who m. 1807,
Harriet, youngest dau. and co-heir of Gustavus Ducarel, of Walford,
Somerset, and d. 24 Apr. 1862. She d. 24 Sept. 1813.   (B.L.G. 18th
ed.)

STAPLEFORD
1. Dexter background black
Argent a chevron between three roundels gules (Sherard), impaling,
Qly, 1st and 4th, Or an eagle displayed sable (Mercia), 2nd and 3rd,
Argent two bars sable each charged with three martlets or (Temple)
Earl's coronet   Crest: From a ducal coronet or a peacock's tail
proper   Motto: Hostis honori invidia   Supporters: Two rams
argent armed and unguled or
For Robert, 6th Earl of Harborough, who m. 1843, Mary Eliza, dau. of
Edward Temple, and d. 28 July 1859.   (B.E.P.)

STAUNTON HAROLD
1. Sinister background black
Qly of twelve, 1st, Ply of six or and azure a quarter ermine, the Badge
of Ulster (Shirley), 2nd, Barry of eight or and azure (   ), 3rd, Gules
a chevron argent between three garbs or (Waldsheafe), 4th, Azure a lion
rampant between eight cross crosslets or (Braose), 5th, Or three piles in
point gules, on a canton argent a griffin segreant sable (Bassett), 6th,
Vairy argent and sable a canton gules (Staunton), 7th, Argent three
wolves passant in pale sable (Lovett), 8th, Argent a fess and in chief

three roundels gules (Devereux), 9th, Argent a cross engrailed gules between four water bougets sable (Bourchier), 10th, Gules billetty or a fess argent (Louvain), 11th, Qly France and England a bordure argent (Plantagenet), 12th, Argent two bars and in chief three molets gules (Washington), impaling, Qly, 1st, Azure a chevron between three hanks of cotton argent (Cotton), 2nd, Or an eagle's leg erased, on a chief indented azure a molet between two roundels argent (Torbuck), 3rd, Argent a chevron sable between three leaves vert a chief sable (Shabery), 4th, Gules a chevron between three owls proper (Sleigh)
Countess's coronet   Motto: Honor virtutis
praemium   Supporters: Dexter, A talbot ermine eared gules ducally gorged or   Sinister, A reindeer gules billetty, attired and ducally gorged or, a horseshoe argent pendent below coronet
For Catherine, dau. of Rowland Cotton, of Etwall, who m. 1754, Robert, 6th Earl Ferrers, and d. 16 Mar. 1786. He d. 17 Apr. 1787.   (B.P. 1949 ed.)

2. Dexter background black
Qly of eight, 1st, Shirley, but no Badge of Ulster, 2nd, Devereux, 3rd, Vairy or and gules (Ferrers), 4th, Azure a wolf's head erased argent (Hugh Lupus, Earl of Chester), 5th, Bourchier, 6th, Plantagenet, 7th, Azure a bend argent cotised or between six lions rampant or (Bohun), 8th, Washington, impaling, Per chevron azure and or, in base an eagle displayed sable on a chief embattled or three roundels gules (Weston)
Viscount's coronet   Crest: A Saracen's head couped at the neck proper wreathed at the temples or and azure   Motto: Malgre l'envie   Supporters: Dexter, as 1., but gorged gules   Sinister, as 1. but no horseshoe   All on a mantle gules and ermine   Skull below
For Robert, Viscount Tamworth, who m. 1821, Anne (d. 7 Oct. 1839), dau. of Richard Weston, and d. 3 Feb. 1830.   (B.P. 1949 ed.)

3. All black background
Qly, 1st and 4th, Shirley, 2nd and 3rd, Plantagnet, impaling, Chequy argent and azure a bend ermine (Ward)
Earl's coronet   Crest and mantle: As 2.   Motto: As 1.   Two badges: To dexter of crest, A horseshoe   To sinister of crest, A Bourchier knot   Supporters: Dexter, A talbot argent, eared gules, ducally gorged or   Sinister, A reindeer gules, billetty argent, ducally gorged or   Each supporter has horseshoe argent below coronet
For Washington, 8th Earl Ferrers, who m. 1st, 1781, Frances (d. 4 Mar. 1812), only dau. of the Rev. William Ward, and 2nd, 1829, Sarah (d. 30 June 1835), dau. of William Davy, and d. 2 Oct. 1842.   (B.P. 1949 ed.)

4. Dexter background black
Qly, 1st and 4th, Shirley, 2nd and 3rd, Plantagenet, the Badge of Ulster in chief between 1st and 2nd qrs., impaling, Qly, 1st and 4th, Chequy or and gules a chief vair (Chichester), 2nd and 3rd, Azure fretty argent (Itchingham)
Earl's coronet   Crest: As 2.   Motto: As 1.   Supporters:
Dexter, as 1.   Sinister, A reindeer gules, billetty and ducally gorged or, attired sable, and charged on the shoulder with a horseshoe argent
For Washington, 9th Earl Ferrers, who m. 1844, Augusta Annabella, dau. of Edward, 4th Marquess of Donegall, and d. 13 Mar. 1859.   (B.P. 1949 ed.)

STOCKERSTON
1. All black background
Chequy or and azure on each square an ermine spot counterchanged, on a chevron gules three escallops argent (Walker)
Crest: A pilgrim's head affronté couped at the shoulders, on the hat and cape proper three escallops argent   Mantling: Azure and or   Motto: Ne cede malis
Unidentified

SWINFORD
1. All black background
Two oval shields   Dexter, Argent a pile sable a chevron counterchanged (Otway)   In pretence: Qly of 35, as sinister shield   Sinister, Qly of 35, 1st, Azure fretty argent (Cave), 2nd, Sable on a bend flory or three escallops gules (Bromflete), 3rd, Ermine on a bend sable three whales' heads erased argent (Whalley?), 4th, Argent a chevron between three popinjays vert (Cliffe?), 5th, Gules a chevron between three molets of six points or (Danvers), 6th, Argent on a bend gules three martlets or winged vert (Danvers), 7th, Argent on a bend gules three chevrons or (Boteler), 8th, Argent on a fess between three martlets sable three molets argent (Pury), 9th, Sable on a fess argent between three anchors or three lions' heads erased gules (Wenman), 10th, Azure on a cross argent five molets gules (Verney), 11h, Azure two chevrons or, on a canton argent a Paschal Lamb couchant gules (   ), 12th, Argent a fess vert, over all a lion rampant gules (Whittingham), 13th, Argent a saltire engrailed sable, on a chief sable two molets argent (Inwardby), 14th, Or on a cross engrailed gules a plain cross sable, in the first quarter a chough proper (Mussenden?), 15th, Argent two bars and in chief a lion passant guardant azure (Frome), 16th, Gules fretty argent on a chief or a lion passant guardant gules (Spigornal), 17th, Azure crusilly and a lion rampant or charged on the shoulder with a fleur-de-lys gules (Braose), 18th, Barry, vairy argent and gules, and azure (Bruce), 19th, Gules two bends, the upper or the lower argent (Milo, Earl of Hereford), 20th, Gules three fusils conjoined in fess or (Newmarch?), 21st, Or two lions passant guardant gules (   ), 22nd, Vair three bends gules (Braye), 23rd, Argent three eagles' legs erased sable armed or (Braye), 24th, Or on a bend gules

three goats passant argent (Hallighwell), 25th, Sable a chevron between
three bulls' heads cabossed argent (Norbury), 26th, Gules a fess
compony counter-compony argent and sable between three crosses formy
fitchy at the foot argent (Boteler), 27th, Gules two bars ermine
(Pantulf), 28th, Or fretty gules (Verdon), 29th, ?Sable a bend between
two lions passant in bend argent? (   ), 30th, Or two bends gules
(Sudeley), 31st, Or four bends azure (Mountfort), 32nd, Argent billetty
a lion rampant sable crowned or (?De la Plaunche), 33rd, Azure a fess
between six cross crosslets argent (Haversham), 34th, Sable a cross
between four bees volant or (Croyser), 35th, Azure a chevron or
(Dabernon)
Baroness's coronet   Supporters: Two lions guardant or with wings
endorsed vair
For Sarah, Baroness Braye, only dau. of Sir Thomas Cave, 6th Bt., who
m. 1790, Henry Otway, and d. 21 Feb. 1862.   (B.P. 1949 ed.)

2. All black background
On a lozenge surmounted by a countess's coronet
Qly, 1st, Gules a chevron engrailed or ermined sable between three
lions' heads erased ermine ducally crowned or (Lygon), 2nd, Argent two
lions passant fork-tailed in pale gules (Lygon), 3rd, Gules three lions
passant in pale argent (?Gifford), 4th, Gules a fess between six martlets
or (Beauchamp)   In pretence: Qly of six, 1st, qly. i. & iv. Azure
fretty argent (Cave), ii. & iii. Argent a pile sable a chevron
counterchanged (Otway), 2nd, Azure fretty argent (Cave), 3rd, Azure on
a cross argent five molets gules (Verney), 4th, Vair three bendlets gules
(Braye), 5th, Argent a chevron between three eagles' legs erased sable
armed gules (Braye), 6th, Or on a bend gules three goats passant or
(Hallighwell)
Supporters: Dexter, A bear proper, muzzled, collared and chained or, on
the breast suspended from the collar an escutcheon, Gules a fess
between six martlets or   Sinister, A swan argent, wings endorsed
gules, beaked and legged sable, gorged with a ducal coronet and lined
or, on the breast suspended from the coronet an escutcheon as dexter
For Catherine, 3rd dau. and co-heiress of Sarah, Baroness Braye, who m.
2nd, John Reginald, 3rd Earl Beauchamp, and d. 21 Jan.
1853.   (B.P. 1949 ed.)

3. All black background
Qly, 1st and 4th, Sable a fess dancetty argent between three eagles
displayed or, a chief or (Wyatt), 2nd and 3rd, Argent on a chevron sable
between three cinquefoils gules three bezants (Edgell)   In pretence
(ensigned with a baroness's coronet): Qly, 1st and 4th, qly i. & iv. Azure
fretty argent (Cave), ii. & iii. Argent a pile sable a chevron
counterchanged (Otway), 2nd and 3rd, Argent a chevron between three
eagles' legs erased sable (Braye)
Two crests: Dexter, A demi-lion per pale embattled or and sable
holding an arrow barbed and flighted or   Sinister, A demi-lion or

holding a cinquefoil gules   Mantling: Sable and argent, with gold
tassels   Motto: Honesta bona
For the Rev. Edgell Wyatt-Edgell, who m. 1844, Henrietta, Baroness
Braye, and d. 26 Sept. 1888, aged 87.   (B.P. 1949 ed.)
(There are duplicates of all these three hatchments in the parish church
at Stanford-on-Avon, Northants)

SWITHLAND

1. All black background
Qly, 1st and 4th, Gules a chevron between three molets pierced or
(Danvers), 2nd and 3rd, Gules on a saltire argent an annulet sable
(Nevill), impaling, Vert an oak tree eradicated argent (Morewood)
Crest: A wyvern or and gules   Mantling: Gules and argent
For John Danvers, who m. Elizabeth (née Morewood), widow of Samuel
Danvers, and d.   (Burke's Commoners I, 149)

2. Dexter background black
Qly, as 1., with Badge of Ulster, impaling, Argent ten roundels, four,
three, two and one gules a label of three points azure (Babington)
Crest: A wyvern or   Mantling: Gules and argent   Motto: Never
fear
For Sir Joseph Danvers, 1st Bt., who m. Frances, dau. of Thomas
Babington, of Rothley Temple, and d. 21 Oct. 1753.   (B.E.B.)

3. All black background
On a lozenge   Arms: As 2.
For Frances, widow of Sir Joseph Danvers, 1st Bt. She d. 4 Feb. 1759.

4. Sinister background black
Qly, 1st and 4th, Gules a chevron wavy between three molets of six
points radiant or pierced azure (Danvers), 2nd and 3rd, Argent three
covered cups between two bends engrailed sable (Butler), impaling,
Vert three bars ermine in chief two roundels argent over all a lion
rampant gules (Fremantle)
Countess's coronet   Supporters: Dexter, A cockatrice vert, beaked or,
ducally gorged or   Sinister, A wyvern, ducally gorged and chained
or, langued gules
For Frances Arabella, 3rd dau. of Col. Stephen Francis William
Fremantle, who m. 1815, as his 1st wife, George John, 5th Earl of
Lanesborough, and d. 5 Oct. 1850.   (B.P. 1939 ed.)

5. Dexter background black
Qly, as 4., impaling, Ermine on a bend cotised vert three bezants
(Bishop)
Earl's coronet   Two crests: Dexter, A wyvern vert, wings and breast
gules and or, ducally gorged and chained or   Sinister, A demi-
cockatrice vert, wings and breast gules and or, ducally gorged

or   Motto: Liberte, toute, entiere   Supporters: Dexter, A
cockatrice, as crest   Sinister, A wyvern, as crest
For George John, 5th Earl of Lanesborough, who m. 2nd, 1851,
Frederica Emma, youngest dau. of Charles Bishop, procurator general to
King George III, and d. 7 July 1866.   (B.P. 1939 ed.)

6. All black background
On a lozenge   Arms: As 5.
Countess's coronet   Supporters: As 5.
For Frederica Emma, widow of George John, 5th Earl of Lanesborough.
She d. 3 Oct. 1870.   (B.P. 1949 ed.)

TUGBY
1. Dexter background black
Qly of six, 1st and 6th, Sable a wolf salient or in chief a fleur-de-lys
argent between two bezants (Wilson), 2nd, Argent a bend and a bordure
engrailed sable (Knyvet), 3rd, Argent a cross engrailed gules between
four water bougets sable a label of three points sable each point charged
with a lion rampant or (Bourchier), 4th, Qly France and England a
bordure argent (Plantagenet) 5th, Qly or and vert (Berners)   In
pretence: Gules a chevron between three quartrefoils argent
(Crump)   Also impaling, Gules a garb or in chief two esquires'
helmets proper garnished or (Cholmondeley)
Baron's coronet   Crest: A demi-wolf rampant or   Motto:
Resurgam   Supporters: Dexter, A falcon rising argent jessed and
belled or   Sinister, A greyhound proper gorged with a collar gules
studded or
For Henry William, 11th Baron Berners, who m. 1st, 1823, Mary Letitia
(d. 30 Sept. 1856), dau. and co-heir of Col. George Crump, of Alexton
Hall, and 2nd, 1857, Henrietta Charlotte (d. 13 Aug. 1874), only dau. of
Thomas, 1st Baron Delamere, and d. 27 June 1871.   (B.P. 1949 ed.)

TWYCROSS
1. Dexter background black
Qly of six, 1st, Argent on a bend sable three popinjays or collared gules
(Curzon), 2nd, Argent on a fess sable three bezants (Penn), 3rd, Argent
a molet pierced sable (Assheton), 4th, Argent two lions passant
guardant azure (Hanmer), 5th, Argent a chevron between three
plummets sable (Jennens), 6th, Or a fess between three wolves' heads
erased sable (Howe)   Shield surrounded with the collar of the
Royal Hanoverian Order, with cross of this and another Order pendent
below   To the sinister of this shield another shield with the same
arms, impaling, Gules a fess argent between six cross crosslets fitchy or
(Gore)
Earl's coronet   Two crests: Dexter, Out of a ducal coronet or a
panache of five ostrich feathers azure   Sinister, A popinjay rising or,
beaked legged and collared gules   Motto: Let Curzon hold what

Curzon held   Supporters: Dexter, A cockatrice or the tail nowed
with a head at the end   Sinister, A chough proper collared with a
chain or
For Richard, 1st Earl Howe, m. 2nd, 1845, Anne (d. 23 July 1877), 2nd
dau. of Admiral Sir John Gore, K.C.B., and d. 12 May 1870.   (B.P.
1949 ed.)

WILLESLEY
1. Dexter background black
Two shields   Dexter, within the Order of Hanover, Argent a
maunch within a bordure engrailed sable, in chief the Badge of Ulster
(Hastings)   Sinister, Hastings.   In within pretence, Or on a
chief gules a demi-lion argent (Abney)
Crest: A bull's head erased sable ducally gorged and armed
or   Motto: In veritate victoria   Supporters: Two Bengal tigers
reguardant proper murally gorged or   All on a mantle azure and
ermine
For Lt.-Gen. Sir Charles Hastings, Bt., who m. Parnell, dau. and heir of
Thomas Abney, of Willesley Hall, and d. 30 Sept. 1823.   (B.P.
1859 ed.)

2. All black background
On a lozenge extending to frame
Hastings, in chief the Badge of Ulster   In pretence: Abney
For Parnell, widow of Lt.-Gen. Sir Charles Hastings, Bt. She d. 11 Feb.
1834, aged 78.   (M.I.)

3. All black background
Qly, 1st and 4th, Hastings, 2nd and 3rd, Abney, over all the Badge of
Ulster
Knight's helm, with chapeau only, and a crest on either
side   Dexter, A bull's head erased sable armed and ducally gorged
argent (Hastings)   Sinister, A demi-lion rampant or resting the
sinister paw on an antique shield charged with the arms of Hastings
(Abney)   Motto: In veritate victoria   Motto: (above helm)
Fortiter et honeste   Supporters: Two lions rampant, the dexter
guardant, or
A very small hatchment, *c.* 18 in. by 18 in.
For Sir Charles Abney-Hastings, 2nd Bt., of Willesley Hall, who d.
unm. 30 July 1858.   (B.P. 1949 ed.; M.I.)

4. Identical to 3., but of normal size and no Badge of Ulster
Perhaps also for Sir Charles Abney-Hastings, 2nd Bt., who d. unm. 30
July 1858.

5. Identical to No. 7 at Ashby-de-la-Zouch
For Edith Maud, Countess of Loudoun, who d. 23 Jan. 1874.   (B.P. 1949 ed.)

WISTOW

1. All black background
Two shields   Dexter, within the Order of Hanover, Argent a greyhound passant sable, on a chief azure a rose argent between two fleurs-de-lys or, on a canton ermine a staff entwined with a serpent proper and ensigned with a coronet or composted of crosses formy and fleurs-de-lys, the Badge of Ulster (Halford)   Sinister, as dexter, impaling, Argent on a chief gules three pierced molets or (St John)
Crests: Dexter, A staff as in the arms   Sinister, A greyhound's head couped sable collared or   Motto: Mutas inglorius artes   Supporters: Two emus proper each gorged with a coronet composted of crosses formy and fleurs-de-lys or
For Sir Henry Vaughan Halford, 1st Bt., physician to George III, who m. 1796, Elizabeth Barbara, 2nd dau. of John, 11th Baron St John, and d. 9 Mar. 1844.   (B.P. 1949 ed.)

RUTLAND*

EDITH WESTON
1. Dexter background black
Argent a chevron between three roundels gules, on a chief azure a cock argent between two cross crosslets fitchy or (Lucas), impaling, Argent two chevronels gules between in chief three estoiles gules and in base a lion rampant sable (Costobadie)

Crest: An arm embowed sleeved sable bezanty cuffed argent holding a cross crosslet fitchy gules   Mantling: Gules and argent   Motto: Resurgam

For Richard Lucas, J.P. of Edith Weston, who m. 1796, Mary, 2nd dau. of the Rev. Joseph Costobadie, Rector of Wensley, and d. 13 Feb. 1846.   (B.L.G. 18th ed.; M.I.)

EMPINGHAM
1. All black background
Qly of eight, 1st, Per pale indented sable and ermine a chevron gules fretty or (Mackworth), 2nd, Azure a cross moline or (De Basings), 3rd, Gules a fess double cotised argent (de Normanville), 4th, Gules a chief argent (Hercy), 5th, Argent on a saltire engrailed sable nine annulets or (Leke), 6th, Argent three fleurs-de-lys between eight cross crosslets fitchy gules (Talbot), 7th, Ermine two bars sable each charged with three molets or (Hopton), 8th, Sable on a chevron argent three pheons sable (   ), the Badge of Ulster

Crest: A sinister wing elevated per pale indented ermine and sable   Mantling: Gules and argent

Probably for Sir Thomas Mackworth, 4th Bt., of Normanton and Empingham, who d. unm. Feb. 1744/5.   (Complete Baronetage)

LYDDINGTON, The Bedehouse
1. All black background
Qly of twenty, 1st, Barry of ten argent and azure six escutcheons three, two and one sable each charged with a lion rampant argent (Cecil), 2nd, Per pale gules and azure a lion rampant argent supporting a tree eradicated vert (Winston), 3rd, Sable three towers tripletowered argent in centre point a roundel argent (Caerleon), 4th, Argent on a bend cotised gules three cinquefoils or (Heckington), 5th, Argent a chevron sable ermined argent between three chessrooks sable (Walcot), 6th, Gules a saltire argent an annulet for difference (Neville), 7th, Lozengy or and gules on a canton argent a ship sable (Neville), 8th, Gules a fess

*See page 57 for Introduction.

between six cross crosslets fitchy or (Beauchamp), 9th, Chequy or and
azure a chevron ermine (Warwick), 10th, Gules a chevron between ten
crosses formy argent (Berkeley), 11th, Gules a lion passant guardant
argent crowned or (De Lysle), 12th, Or a fess between two chevrons
sable (Lisle), 13th, Argent a cross engrailed gules between four water
bougets sable (Bourchier), 14th, Qly France and England within a
bordure argent (Plantagenet), 15th, Gules two bendlets the upper one or
the lower argent (Fitzwater), 16th, Qly or and vert (Berners), 17th, Qly
gules and or a molet argent (Vere), 18th, Sable a lion rampant argent
gutty gules (?de Verdon), 19th, Gules on a bend between six cross
crosslets fitchy argent in dexter chief an ermine spot (?Howard), 20th,
Or a chevron gules and a bordure engrailed sable (Stafford)   In
pretence and impaling, Or an inescutcheon within an orle of martlets
sable (Brownlow)
Earl's coronet   Crest: On a chapeau gules and ermine a garb or
supported by two lions the dexter argent the sinister
azure   Mantling: Gules and ermine   Motto: Cor unum via
una   Supporters: Two lions ermine
For John, 6th Earl of Exeter, who m. 2nd, 1699, Elizabeth (d. 28 Nov.
1723), dau. and co-heir of Sir John Brownlow, Bt., and d. 24 Dec.
1721.   (B.P. 1949 ed.)
(In view of the background possibly also used by his widow)

2. All black background
Qly of twenty, as 1., but with the following differences, 5th, Argent a
chevron between three chessrooks sable ermined argent (Walcot), 7th,
Or fretty gules on a canton argent a ship sable (Neville), 18th, Vert a
lion rampant argent vulned in the shoulder proper (De Verdon)
Earl's coronet   Crest: As 1., but no chapeau   Mantling, motto
and supporters: As 1.
For John, 7th Earl of Exeter, who d. unm. 9 Apr. 1722.   (B.P. 1949
ed.)

3. All black background
Qly of six, 1st and 6th, Cecil, 2nd, Winston, 3rd, Caerleon, 4th,
Heckington, 5th, Walcot, as 2.
Earl's coronet   Crest: As 1., but dexter lion azure, sinister
argent   Mantling, motto and supporters: As 1.
Unidentified

MORCOTT
1. Dexter background black
Qly, 1st and 4th, Argent on a bend sable between two choughs proper
three escallops argent (Rowley), 2nd and 3rd, Sable a chevron between
three escallops argent (   )   In pretence: Qly, 1st and 4th, qly
i. & iv. Gules a fess chequy argent and azure (Lindsay), ii. & iii. Or a
lion rampant debruisd by a bendlet sable (Abernethy), all within a

bordure azure semy of molets or, 2nd, Argent two bars gemel azure in chief two martlets respectant azure in base a lion passant guardant gules (Fydell), 3rd, Or three garbs gules (   )
Crests: Dexter, A molet pierced argent   Sinister, Out of the rays of the sun gules a demi-lion ducally gorged gules holding in its paws an escutcheon or charged with an anchor sable   Mantling: Azure and argent   Motto: Resurgam
For George Dawson Rowley, of Morcott Hall, who m. 1849, Caroline Frances, only child of Archdeacon Lindsay, and d. 21 Nov. 1878.   (B.L.G. 1937 ed.)

2. All black background
On a lozenge surrounded by scrollwork
Rowley   In pretence: Qly, 1st and 4th, Lindsay, 2nd and 3rd, Abernethy
For Caroline Frances, widow of George Dawson Rowley, d. 3 Jan. 1900.   (B.L.G. 1937 ed.)

TICKENCOTE
1. Dexter background black
Argent on a bend gules cotised sable three pairs of wings conjoined argent (Wingfield), impaling, Argent a water bouget sable, on a chief azure three annulets or (Johnson)
Crest: A cap per pale sable gutty or and argent banded gules between two wings expanded dexter or, sinister sable gutty or   Motto: Posse nolle nobile
For John Harry Lee Wingfield, of Tickencote Hall, who m. 1861, Elizabeth Anne, eldest dau. of Maurice Johnson, of Ayscoughfee Hall, Lincs, and d. 22 Feb. 1880.   (B.L.G. 1937 ed.)

TIXOVER
1. All black background
On a lozenge surmounted by a cherub's head and surrounded by scrollwork   Or a fret azure (Eaton), impaling, Or a bend between three leopards' faces azure (Waldie)
For Charlotte Anne, dau. of George Waldie, of Hendersyde Park, Roxburgh, who m. Stephen Eaton, of Ketton Hall, and d. 28 Sept. 1859.   (B.L.G. 1871 ed.; M.I.)

WHISSENDINE
1. All black background
Argent a chevron between three roundels gules (Sherard)   In pretence: Sable three lozenges argent on a chief or three fleurs-de-lys gules (Pedley)

Earl's coronet   Motto: Hostis honori invidia   Supporters: Two
rams argent armed and unguled or
For Philip, 2nd Earl of Harborough, who m. Anne, dau. and heir of
Nicholas Pedley, and d. 20 July 1750.   (Complete Peerage)

LINCOLNSHIRE

by

Henry Thorold, F.S.A.

Doddington 1: For John Hussey, 1st Baron Delaval, 1808
(*Photograph by Mr. P. Burton*)

INTRODUCTION

It is perhaps disappointing that in a county so large as Lincolnshire there are only 125 hatchments; it is disappointing, too, that none survive of the great families of the Dukes and Earls of Ancaster, of the Earls of Yarborough, of the Brownlows or the Heneages. But most of the other ancient county families are represented, and it is cheering to note that the majority of these families still survive in the county; indeed a word of appreciation is due to their representatives today who have generously helped with the checking of their forbears' arms and the identification of their hatchments.

The oldest hatchment which can be identified and dated is that of George Lucas (d. 1690), at Marston: it bears the arms of Lucas of Fenton, impaling those of his wife Penelope, daughter of Sir William Thorold, 1st Bt. of Marston. The latest hatchment is also at Marston, and is that of Dorothy Frances Thorold, who died in 1969. Other early hatchments are those at Asgarby, bearing the arms of Rowe, and at Norton Disney, with the arms of Barnard; but these can neither be dated nor firmly identified.

There are nine hatchments at Spalding all connected with the family of that attractive character Maurice Johnson, founder of the Spalding Gentlemen's Society; and eight at Boston, four of which are of the Fydell family, talented and wealthy merchants of Boston, who built Fydell House, the most distinguished 18th-century building in the town. The largest family collection is that of the Welbys, baronets of Denton, with seven hatchments. Three of them are complicated and many-quartered, and, like great patchwork quilts, hang in a dark position under the tower to fox the hatchment-spotter of today.

At Redbourne hang hatchments of Dukes of St Albans, descendants of Charles II and Nell Gwynn, displaying the Royal Arms of the Stuarts, debruised by the baton sinister; at Baumber hatchments of Fynes-Clinton and Pelham-Clinton,

89

Earls of Lincoln and Dukes of Newcastle, remind us that this family in the early 18th century were buried in Lincolnshire. Equally the Saunderson-Lumley hatchments at Saxby St Helen recall that the Earls of Scarbrough in the 18th and 19th centuries treated that little Georgian church as their mausoleum. The two Delaval hatchments at Doddington record the connection of that great house with Seaton Delaval in Northumberland.

Perhaps the most attractive set in the county is that of the five little hatchments of Batemans, Dashwoods and Chaplins which adorn the gallery of the 18th-century church at Well. Two Monson hatchments at South Carlton are repeated in the neighbouring family church at Burton. The hatchment of Sir Henry Hickman Bacon, Premier Baronet of England, which hangs in Gainsborough Old Hall, is accompanied by an old photograph of the hatchment hanging over the front door at Thonock, the Bacon seat just outside the town.

The first hatchment that I ever saw hanging over a door was that of Dr. M. R. James, Provost of Eton: I was a boy in the school at the time. Reading his celebrated ghost story *Lost Hearts*, its scene set at Aswarby Hall 'in the heart of Lincolnshire', sent me bicycling over in the holidays to Aswarby, where in the church I found the hatchments of the Whichcotes, baronets of Aswarby – the first hatchments I ever (consciously) saw in a church. So was born an interest in the subject which prompted me to set up the hatchment here for my mother in 1969.

Finally it remains to pay tribute to Mr. A. E. Lloyd and to the late Mr. J. Tindale, whose painstaking recordings of Lincolnshire hatchments form the basis of this survey; and to Mr. Ray Elliott who, in recent years, has been responsible for a number of additions and amendments.

Henry Thorold, F.S.A.,
Marston Hall, Grantham

ASGARBY

1. All black background

On a lozenge Gules on a bend between three garbs or three crosses formy fitchy sable (Rowe)

A small hatchment, *c.* 2 ft. by 2 ft.

Unidentified

ASHBY-DE-LA-LAUNDE

1. All black background

Sable on a chevron argent three escallops sable (King), impaling, Argent a chevron between three foxes' heads erased gules (Fox)

Crest: A talbot's head couped sable Mantling: Gules and ermine Motto: Virtuti fortuna cedit

For Capt. John King, of Ashby Hall, who m. Millicent Mary, dau. of John Fox, of Rowston, Lincs, and d. 1793. She d. 1792. (Lincs. Peds.)

ASWARBY

1. Sinister background black

Ermine two boars passant gules in chief (over line of impalemnt), the Badge of Ulster (Whichcote), impaling, Sable ermined argent on a cross quarterpierced argent four millrinds sable (Turnor)

Motto: Resurgam Two cherubs' heads above shield

For Diana, 3rd dau. of Edmund Turnor of Stoke Rochford, who m. 1785, Sir Thomas Whichcote, 5th Bt., and d. 4 Feb. 1826. (B.P. 1949 ed.)

2. All black background

Arms: As 1., with Badge of Ulster in chief on Whichcote coat

Crest: A boar's head erased and erect gules Mantling: Gules and argent Motto: Resurgam

For Sir Thomas Whichcote, 5th Bt., who d. 22 Sept. 1828. (B.P. 1949 ed.)

3. Sinister background black

Whichcote, with Badge of Ulster in fess (over line of impalement), impaling, Gules a fess or ermined sable between three boars' heads couped or (Beckett)

Mantling: Gules and argent Motto: Resurgam

For Marianne, only dau. of Henry Beckett, who m. 1839, as his 1st wife, Sir Thomas Whichcote, 7th Bt., and d. 10 May 1849. (B.P.)

AUBOURN

1. Dexter background black

Gules a saltire ermine (Nevile), impaling, Sable three lions passant
between two double cotises argent in chief a crescent argent for difference
(Browne)
Crest: From a ducal coronet or a bull's head argent armed
or   Mantling: Gules and argent   Motto: Ne vile
For Christopher Nevile, of Wellingore, who m. 1st, Elizabeth Sharp, and
2nd, Miss Brown, and d. 14 Jan. 1772, aged 60.   (B.L.G. 1937 ed.;
M.I.)

2. Sinister background black

Nevile, impaling, Or fretty gules a canton ermine (Noel)
Crest: From a ducal coronet or a bull's head argent   Mantling and
motto: As 1.
For Sophia, dau. of Henry, 4th Earl of Gainsborough, who m.
Christopher Nevile, of Wellingore, and d. 5 May 1780.   (B.L.G.
1937 ed.; M.I.)

BAUMBER

1. All black background

Two shields   Dexter, within the Garter, Argent six cross crosslets
fitchy, three, two and one sable, on a chief azure two molets or
(Clinton)   Sinister, Clinton, with in pretence, Qly, 1st and 4th,
Azure three pelicans vulning themselves argent (Pelham), 2nd and 3rd,
Ermine two piles sable (Holles)
Duke's coronet   Crest: From a ducal coronet or five ostrich feathers
argent   Mantling: Gules and argent   Motto: Loyalte n'a
honte   Supporters: Two greyhounds argent collared gules
For Henry, 2nd Duke of Newcastle, K.G., who m. 1744, Catherine,
eldest dau. of the Rt. Hon. Henry Pelham, and d. 22 Feb.
1794.   (B.P. 1949 ed.)

2. Dexter background black

Qly, 1st and 4th, Clinton (molets pierced gules), 2nd and 3rd, qly i. &
iv. Azure three pelicans vulning themselves proper (Pelham), ii. & iii.
Gules two pieces of belt in pale buckles in chief argent (Pelham),
impaling, Qly, 1st and 4th, Sable on a bend cotised argent a rose gules
between two annulets sable (Conway), 2nd and 3rd, qly i. & iv. Or on a
pile gules between six fleurs-de-lys azure three lions passant guardant or
(Seymour), ii. & iii. Gules a pair of wings conjoined and inverted or
(Seymour)
Earl's coronet   Crest: From a ducal coronet gules a plume of five
ostrich feathers argent   Mantle: Gules and ermine   Motto and
supporters: As 1.
For Henry Fiennes, Earl of Lincoln, who m. 1775, Frances, dau. of
Francis, Earl of Hertford, and d. 22 Oct. 1778.   (B.P. 1949 ed.)

3. All black background
Qly, as dexter of 2.
Earl's coronet   Crest, motto and supporters: As 2.   Mantling:
Gules and argent
Probably for Henry Pelham, Earl of Clinton, only son of 2. who died 23
Sept. 1779 aged under 2 years.   (Complete Peerage)

4. Dexter background black
Qly, 1st and 4th, Argent a lion rampant gules between three trefoils
slipped vert (Livesey), 2nd and 3rd, Or on a bend azure between six
cross crosslets sable three garbs argent (Bancroft), impaling, Azure on a
bend wavy or three birds proper a bordure argent (Reade)
Crest: A lion's gamb erased gules holding five trefoils
vert   Mantling: Gules and argent   Motto: In coelo quies
For Joseph Livesey, who m. 1811, Ann, dau. of George Reade, and d. 21
June 1843. She d. 15 Oct. 1877.   (M.I.)

5. Dexter background black
Qly, as 4, impaling, Sable a fess between three fleurs-de-lys argent
(Welby)
Crest, mantling and motto: As 4.
For Joseph Livesey, of Stourton Hall, who m. 1850, Sarah Maria, dau.
of the Rev. John Earle Welby, of Harston, Leics, and d. 19 Jan.
1854.   (M.I.; B.L.G. 5th ed.)

6. Sinister background black
On a lozenge   Arms: As 5.
Mantling: Gules and argent
For Sarah Maria, wife of Joseph Livesey, who d. 16 Jan.
1854.   (Sources, as 5.)
(On this hatchment and on No. 5. there are errors in that, if the dates on
the monument are correct, the background off his hatchment should have
been all black and her arms should not have been on a lozenge)

BINBROOK
1. All black background
Qly, 1st and 4th, Per fess gules and azure two cats-a-mountain passant
guardant in pale argent spotted sable, on a canton or a cross crosslet
fitchy sable (Caton), 2nd and 3rd, Qly gules and vair on a bend or an
annulet and a crescent in chief sable (Constable), impaling, Argent a
bend engrailed gules, on a chief gules three escallops argent (Power)
No helm   Crests: Dexter, Out of a castle argent charged with three
cross crosslets fitchy sable a Saracen's head and shoulders affronté
proper wreathed at the temples or and gules   Sinister, A stag's head
cabossed proper between the antlers or a cross or   Mantling: Gules
and argent   Mottoes: (above crests) Per crucem ad
coronam   (below shield) Cautus metuit foveam

For the Rev. Richard Bewley Caton, who m. 1st, Eliza, dau. of
Redmond Power, of Whitefort, Tipperary, and 2nd, Harriet, dau. of
Clement Harrison, of Bath, and d. 1864.   (B.L.G. 1937 ed.)

BLYBOROUGH
1. Dexter background black
Qly, 1st and 4th, Per pale sable and argent a lion rampant
counterchanged holding in its paws a molet of six points or in chief two
fleurs-de-lys counterchanged (Luard), 2nd and 3rd, Gules a chevron
argent between three molets of six points or (Bourryau), impaling, Per
fess gules and or, in base an olive tree eradicated and fructed proper in
chief the head and forelegs of a crocodile issuant proper (Dalbiac)
Crest: A demi-lion rampant sable charged with a fleur-de-lys or holding
a molet of six points argent   Mantling: Dexter, Gules and
argent   Sinister, Gules and or   Motto: Prospice
For Peter John Luard, of Blyborough Hall, who m. 1783, Louisa, dau. of
Charles James Dalbiac, of Hungerford Park, Berkshire, and d. 23 May,
1830. She d. 4 Jan. 1831, aged 69.   (B.L.G. 2nd ed.; M.I.)

BOSTON
1. Dexter background black
Argent two bars gemel azure in chief an anchor sable between two
martlets respectant vert and in base a lion passant guardant gules
(Fydell)   In pretence: Argent a chevron between three talbots'
heads erased sable (Hall)
Motto: Vivit post funera virtus   Cherub's head above
For Richard Fydell, M.P. for Boston, 1734, who m. 1739, Elizabeth
Hall, and d. 11 Apr. 1780. She d. 1783.   (B.L.G. 2nd ed.; M.I.)

2. Dexter background black
Qly, 1st and 4th, Fydell as 1., 2nd, Argent a chevron sable between
three lions' heads erased gules (Hall), 3rd, Or a fess embattled between
three Catherine wheels sable (Cartwright)   In pretence: Or three
garbs gules (Preston)
Crest: A demi-lion or collared gules, rising out of the rays of the sun
proper, holding a shield, or an anchor sable   Mantling: Gules and
argent   Motto: Resurgam
For Thomas Fydell, who m. Elizabeth, 2nd dau. of Samuel Preston, and
d. 6 Apr. 1812.   (B.L.G. 2nd ed.)

3. Sinister background black
Qly, as 2., but Fydell arms, two bars not gemel, and Hall arms as 1. In
pretence: Ermine on a bend azure three pheons or (Carleton)
Mantling: Gules and argent   Motto: Spes mea in Deo
        Cherub's head above
For Elizabeth, dau. of Thomas Carleton, who m. as his 1st wife, Samuel
Richard Fydell, and d. 29 Apr. 1816.   (B.L.G. 2nd ed.)

4. All black background
Arms: As 3., but Fydell, as 1., also impaling, Argent two lions passant in pale sable (Browne)
Crest: As 2., but lion argent   Mantling: Azure and argent   Motto: Spes mea in Deo
For Samuel Richard Fydell, who m. 2nd, Elizabeth, dau. of Edward Brown of Stamford, and d. 1868.   (B.L.G. 2nd ed.)

5. Sinister background black
Qly, 1st and 4th, Per chevron gules and sable a chevron between three swans argent beaks and feet or (Michell), 2nd and 3rd, Argent on a fess sable three bucks' heads cabossed or (Hutton)   In pretence: Argent on a chevron between three talbots' heads erased sable a molet of six points or (Hall)
Motto: Memoria pii eterna   Cherub's head above
Unidentified

6. Dexter background black
Or on a cross qly azure and gules a lion passant in chief, two squirrels sejant in fess and an annulet in base or (Pacey)   In pretence: Barry wavy of six argent and sable, on a chief gules a saltire or (Wallington)
Crest: A boar's head erect and couped azure charged with an anchor and a sword in saltire or   Mantling: Gules and argent   Motto: Mors janua vitae
For Henry Butler Pacey, who m. Hannah, dau. and heiress of John Wallington, and d. 24 Jan. 1785, aged 77.   (M.I.; Lincs Peds.)

7. All black background
Qly, 1st, Per bend indented or and azure two crosses formy counterchanged (Smith), 2nd, Gules a chevron between nine cross crosslets or (Kyme), 3rd, Gules on a cross or five molets sable (Randolph), 4th, Argent a doubleheaded eagle sable charged on the breast with a trefoil slipped or (Stukeley)
Unidentified

8. All black background
Qly, 1st, Smith, 2nd, Argent a bear sable muzzled and collared or (Barnard), 3rd, Randolph, 4th, Or three bars sable (   )
Unidentified

BRANSTON
1. Dexter background black
Or three battering rams proper headed azure (Bertie)   In pretence: Sable a chevron between three eagles' heads erased or (Casey)
Crest: A Saracen's head and shoulders proper ducally crowned or   Mantling: Gules and argent   Motto: Loyauté me

oblige   Supporters: Dexter, A friar proper   Sinister, A savage
proper
For Lord Vere Bertie, eldest son of Robert, 1st Duke of Ancaster, who
m. 1736, Anne Casey, illegitimate dau. of Sir Cecil Wray, and d. 13
Sept. 1768.   (B.P. 1949 ed.; M.I.)

2. All black background
On a lozenge   Arms: As 1.
Initials above lozenge AFB   Mantling: Gules and or   Motto
and supporters: As 1.
For Anne, widow of Lord Vere Bertie, d. 13 Nov. 1778.   (Sources, as
1.)
(These two hatchments were destroyed in a fire in 1962)

BURTON
1. Dexter background black
Or two chevronels gules (Monson), impaling, Ermine three leopards'
faces or on a chief gules a lion passant guardant or (Larken)
Baron's coronet   Crest: A lion rampant or supporting a pillar
argent   Motto: Prêt pour mon pays   Supporters: Dexter, A lion
or gorged with a collar and having a line reflexed over the back azure,
the collar charged with three crescents or   Sinister, A griffin, wings
elevated argent, beaked and membered azure, collared and lined as
dexter, but collar uncharged
For William John, 6th Baron Monson, who m. 1828, Eliza, dau. of
Edmund Larken, of Bedford Square, and d. 17 Dec. 1862.   (B.P.
1949 ed.)
(There is another hatchment for Lord Monson at South Carlton, and at
Gatton, Surrey)

2. All black background
On a lozenge surmounted by a baroness's coronet
Arms: As 1.   Supporters: As 1.
For Eliza, widow of William John, 6th Baron Monson, d. 22 Jan.
1863.   (B.P. 1949 ed.)
(There is another hatchment for Lady Monson at South Carlton, and at
Gatton, Surrey)

BURWELL
1. Dexter backgound black
Qly, 1st and 4th, Ermine on a fess sable three molets argent (Lister),
2nd and 3rd, Or on a bend between six cross crosslets sable three garbs
or (Bancroft), impaling, Argent on a chevron gules three lions passant
guardant or (Bolton)
Crest: A stag's head erased proper   Mantling: Gules and
ermine   Motto: Est modus

For Matthew Bancroft Lister, of Burwell Park, who m. 1799, Sophia
Bolton, of London, and d. 14 Oct. 1842.   (B.L.G. 1937 ed.; M.I.)

CANWICK
1. Dexter background black
Qly, 1st and 4th, Argent two bars gules within a bordure engrailed
sable (Sibthorp), 2nd and 3rd, Or a bend azure between three leopards'
faces gules (Waldo), impaling, Gules a chevron argent between three
eagles' heads erased or (Ellison)
Crest: A demi-lion rampant erased argent collared azure, in the dexter
paw a fleur-de-lys azure   Mantling: Gules and argent   Motto:
Resurgam
For Humphrey Waldo-Sibthorp, who m. 1777, Susanna, 2nd dau. of
Richard Ellison, of Thorne, Yorks, and d. 25 Apr. 1815.   (B.L.G.
7th ed.)

2. All black background
On a lozenge   Arms: As 1., but bordure not engrailed and chevron
argent
For Susanna, widow of Humphry Waldo-Sibthorp, d. 12 May 1826; or
perhaps for Mary Esther, elder dau. and co-heiress of Henry Ellison, of
Thorne, Yorks, who m. the Rev. Humphry Waldo-Sibthorp, Rector of
Washingbrough, Lincs, and d. 1875.   (B.L.G. 7th ed.)

3. All black background
Arms: As dexter of 1.
Crests: Two, not clear enough to blazon, but probably Sibthorp and
Waldo
Mantle: Gules and argent   Motto: Nil conscire sibi
For Coningsby Waldo Waldo-Sibthorp, M.P. for Lincoln, who d. unm. 9
Mar. 1822.   (B.L.G. 7th ed.)

4. Dexter background black
Qly, 1st and 4th, Sibthorp as 1., 2nd, Waldo as 1., 3rd, Gules three
conies sejant within a bordure engrailed argent (Coningsby), impaling,
Qly of six, 1st, Gules four barrulets indented argent (Tottenham), 2nd,
Sable a chevron engrailed ermine between three trefoils slipped argent
(Loftus), 3rd, Gyronny of eight sable and argent a saltire engrailed per
saltire between four fleurs-de-lys counterchanged (Loftus), 4th, Or a
chevron gules between three hunting horns sable stringed gules
(Crewkerne), 5th, Argent a fess engrailed sable (   ), 6th, Azure a
chevron between three billets or (   )
Crests: Dexter, A demi-lion rampant erased argent collared azure in its
dexter paw a fleur-de-lys azure   Sinister, A demi-leopard rampant
guardant or charged with two bendlets azure   Mantling: Gules and
argent   Motto: Resurgam

For Charles de Laet Waldo-Sibthorp, who m. 1812, Maria, 3rd dau. and
co-heir of Ponsonby Tottenham, of co. Wexford, and d. 14 Dec.
1855.   (M.I.; B.L.G. 7th ed.)

5. Dexter backgound black
Qly, as dexter of 4., but conies couchant, impaling, Qly, 1st and 4th,
Sable on a bend indented argent three martlets sable (Cracroft), 2nd
and 3rd, Argent a tower between three covered cups sable (Amcotts)
Crests: Dexter, A demi-lion rampant erased argent collared azure in its
dexter paw a fleur-de-lys azure   Sinister, A demi-leopard rampant
or charged with two bendlets azure   Mantle: Gules and
ermine   Motto: Nil conscire sibi
For Gervaise Tottenham Waldo-Sibthorp, J.P., D.L., who m. 1846,
Louisa, 3rd dau. of Robert Cracroft, of Hackthorn, Lincs, and d. 13 Oct.
1861.   (B.L.G. 7th ed.)

SOUTH CARLTON
1. Dexter background black
Or two chevronels gules (Monson), impaling, Argent two battleaxes in
saltire sable (Maddison)
Baron's coronet   Crest: A lion rampant supporting a column
or   Mantling: Gules and argent   Motto: Prest pour mon
pais   Supporters: Dexter, A lion or collared and chained azure, on
the collar three crescents or   Sinister, A griffin argent collared and
chained as dexter
For John, 2nd Baron Monson, who m. Theodosia, dau. of John
Maddison, of Harpswell, Lincs, and d. 1774.   (B.P. 1949 ed.)

2. Dexter background black
Monson, impaling, Argent gutty gules a Danish warrior armed with in
the dexter hand a battleaxe and in the sinister a sword all proper
(Blacker)
Baron's coronet   Crest, motto and supporters: As 1.
For Frederick, 5th Baron Monson, who m. Theodosia, youngest dau. of
Latham Blacker, of Newent, Gloucs, and d.s.p. 7 Oct. 1841.   (B.P.
1949 ed.)
(There is another hatchment for Lord Monson, at Gatton, Surrey)

3. Identical to, but slightly larger than, No. 1. at Burton
For William John, 6th Baron Monson, who m. 1828, Eliza, dau. of
Edmund Larken, of Bedford Square, and d. 17 Dec. 1862.   (B.P.
1949 ed.)
(There is also a hatchment to Lord Monson at Gatton, Surrey)

4. Identical to, but slightly larger than, No. 2. at Burton
For Eliza, widow of William John, 6th Baron Monson, d. 22 Jan.
1863.   (B.P. 1949 ed.)

(There is also a hatchment for Lady Monson at Gatton, Surrey)

COLSTERWORTH

1. Dexter background black
Two coats per pale, 1st, Gules a bend argent billetty sable (Mirehouse),
2nd, Per chevron embattled or and azure three molets counterchanged
(   ), impaling, Per pale azure and gules three lions rampant argent
(Herbert)
Crest: An arm in armour embowed grasping a sword all
proper   Mantling: Gules and argent   Motto: Qualis ab incepto
For the Rev. William Squire Mirehouse, Rector of Colsterworth, who m.
1832, Eliza Brunetta, only dau. of George Arthur Herbert, and d. 26
Mar. 1864.   (B.L.G. 5th ed.)

2. All black background
On a decorative asymmetric lozenge
Arms: As 1.   Mantle: Gules and argent
For Eliza Brunetta, widow of the Rev. William Squire Mirehouse, d.
1874.   (B.L.G. 5th ed.)

CORRINGHAM, Beckett Arms

1. Dexter background black
Gules a fess or ermined sable between three boars' heads couped or, in
chief the Badge of Ulster (Beckett), impaling, Qly, 1st and 4th, Beckett,
2nd and 3rd, Ermine on a fess gules three lions rampant argent (for
Beckett of Barnsley)
Crest: A boar's head couped or pierced by a cross formy fitchy erect
sable   Mantling: Gules and argent   Motto: Prodesse civibus
For Sir Thomas Beckett, 3rd Bt., who m. 1825, Caroline, dau. of Joseph
Beckett, of Barnsley, and d. 17 Nov. 1872.   (B.P. 1875 ed.)

DENTON

1. All black background
Qly, 1st and 4th, Sable a fess between three fleurs-de-lys (Welby), 2nd
and 3rd, Sable a tower or (Towers), impaling, Gules in chief two
helmets proper garnished or in base a garb or (Cholmeley)
Crest: An arm in armour ungauntleted issuing from a cloud proper
holding a short sword proper hilted or over flames
proper   Mantling: Gules and argent   Motto: Mors janua vitae
For William Welby, who m. Catherine, dau. of James Cholmeley, of
Easton, and d. 29 June 1792.   (B.P. 1949 ed.)

2. Dexter background black
Qly of 13, 1st Welby with Badge of Ulster, 2nd and 10th, Barry of six
argent and gules (Moulton), 3rd and 11th, Or an eagle with two heads
displayed sable (Kinsey), 4th and 12th, Azure a saltire between four
cross crosslets or (?Friskney), 5th and 13th, Ermine on a bend gules
three leopards' faces or (?Stinte), 6th, Towers, 7th, Gules three lozenges

argent each charged with an eagle displayed sable (Bishop), 8th, Or a
molet between three pheons sable (   ), 9th, Barry of four argent and
sable a fess gules (   )   In pretence: Argent on a chevron sable
between three roses gules slipped and leaved proper three fleurs-de-lys
argent (Cope)
Crest and mantling: As 1., but no flames on crest   Motto: Per ignem
per gladium
For Sir William Earle Welby, 1st Bt., who m. 2nd, 1773, Elizabeth,
dau. of Robert Cope, of Spondon, Derby, and d. 6 Nov. 1815.   (B.P.
1949 ed.)

3. Sinister background black
Welby, with Badge of Ulster   In pretence: Qly, 1st and 4th, Azure
two bars and in chief a chevron or (Spry), 2nd and 3rd, Per saltire
argent and gules four crescents counterchanged (Spry)
Mantle: Gules and argent
For Wilhelmina, only dau. and heiress of William Spry, Governor of
Barbados, who m. 1792, Sir William Earle Welby, 2nd Bt., and d. 4
Feb. 1847.   (B.P. 1949 ed.)

4. Dexter background black
Qly of 15, 1st and 15th, qly i. & iv. Gules crusilly or on a chevron or
three cross crosslets gules a canton argent (Gregory), ii. & iii. Welby,
over all the badge of Ulster, 2nd, Barry of six argent and gules in chief
three roundels gules (   ), 3rd, Or an eagle with two heads displayed
sable (   ), 4th, Per fess ermine and gules fretty or (   ), 5th,
Azure a saltire between four cross crosslets or (?Friskney), 6th, Ermine
on a bend gules three leopards' faces or (?Stinte), 7th, Towers, 8th, Or a
molet between three pheons sable (   ), 9th, Bishop, as 2., 10th,
Argent on a bend cotised gules three roundels argent (Bishop), 11th, Or
on a chief indented azure three annulets argent (?Hereford), 12th, Welby
with in chief a crescent argent, 13th, Lozengy azure and or a canton
ermine (   ), 14th, Spry qly as 3., impaling, Qly of five, 1st and 5th,
Cholmeley, 2nd, Paly bendy argent and azure a bend gules fretty or
(Cheyney), 3rd, Argent three cocks sable (Pomfret), 4th, Azure on a
chief argent three eagles displayed sable (Harrison)
Crests: Dexter, Three garbs or   Sinister, as 1.   Mantling and
motto: As 2.
For Sir Glynne Earle Welby-Gregory, 3rd Bt., who m. 1828, Frances,
youngest dau. of Sir Montague Cholmeley, 1st Bt., and d. 23 Aug.
1875.   (B.P. 1949 ed.)

5. All black background
Qly of 17, 1st, 11th and 17th, Welby, with Badge of Ulster in 1st
quarter, 2nd and 12th, Barry of six argent and gules (   ), 3rd and
13th, Or an eagle with two heads displayed sable (   ), 4th and 14th,
Gules fretty or a chief ermine (?Fouleshurst), 5th and 15th, Azure a

saltire between four cross crosslets or (?Friskney), 6th and 16th, Ermine on a bend gules three leopards' faces or (?Stinte), 7th, Towers, 8th, Or a molet between three pheons sable (   ), 9th, Spry qly, 10th, Or on a chief indented azure three annulets argent (?Hereford)
Crest: not discernible   Mantling and motto: As 2.
Unidentified

6. All black background

Qly, 1st and 4th, qly i. & iv. Welby, ii. & iii. Towers, 2nd and 3rd, Cholmeley
Crest and mantling: As 1.   Skull and crossbones in base
Unidentified

7. All black background

Welby arms only
Crest: not discernible   Mantling: Gules and argent
Possibly for William Welby of Denton who d. unm. 1704.   (Lincs. Peds.)

(All these hatchments are very difficult to see and so may be inaccurately blazoned)

DODDINGTON
1. Dexter background black

Qly, 1st and 4th, Ermine two bars azure (Delaval), 2nd and 3rd, Argent a chevron between three garbs azure (Blake) over all the Badge of Ulster, impaling, Argent three bends gules within a bordure gules, on a canton azure a spur or (Knight)
Baron's coronet   Mantle: Gules and ermine   Supporters: Two men in armour, dexter holding Magna Charta scroll in right hand and a sword in the left   Motto: Dieu me conduise
For John Hussey, 1st Baron Delaval, who m. 2nd, Susanna Elizabeth Knight, and d. 17 May 1808.   (B.E.P.)
(There is another hatchment for Lord Delaval at Seaton Delaval, Northumberland)

2. Dexter background black

Qly, 1st and 4th, Delaval, 2nd and 3rd, Or a cross vert (Hussey), impaling, Argent on a bend azure three crescents or a bordure engrailed gules (Scott)
Crest: A ram's head erased argent horned or   Mantling: Gules and argent   Motto: Dieu me conduise
For Edward Hussey Delaval, who m. 1808, Sarah, dau. of George Scott, of Methley, and d. 14 Aug. 1814.   (B.E.P.)
(There is another hatchment for Edward Hussey Delaval at Seaton Delaval, Northumberland)

FRISKNEY
1. Dexter background black
Argent three boars heads' erect erased sable (Booth)   In pretence:
Qly of 16, 1st and 16th, Or on a cross qly azure and gules a martlet
between in chief a lion passant argent in fess two squirrels and in base
an annulet or (Pacey), 2nd, Azure a chevron between three covered cups
or (Butler), 3rd, Or a lion rampant vert (   ), 4th, Gules a cinquefoil
ermine (   ), 5th, Or two lions passant sable (   ), 6th, Or a cross
flory sable (   ), 7th, Argent a saltire engrailed gules (   ), 8th,
Argent a fess between two bars gemel gules (Badlesmere), 9th, Or a lion
rampant gules (   ), 10th, Azure semy-de-lys argent a lion rampant
guardant argent (   ), 11th, Gules three lions passant guardant in
pale or a bordure argent (Woodstock), 12th, Argent two bars and in
chief three roundels gules (Wake), 13th, Barry of eight argent and gules
(   ), 14th, Barry wavy of eight argent and sable on a chief gules a
saltire or (Wallington), 15th, Argent a sun in splendour gules (Hurst)
Crest: A lion passant argent   Mantling: Sable and
argent   Motto: Quod ero spero
For the Rev. Thomas Willingham Booth, who m. Mary Anne, dau. and
heiress of William Pacey, and d. 6 Nov. 1869.   (Lincs Peds.)

2. Dexter background black
Booth, impaling, Argent on a bend gules between three lions' heads
erased gules a dolphin between two martlets or (Franklyn)
Crest: A lion passant argent   Mantling: Sable and
argent   Mottoes: (above crest) Quod ero spero   (Below shield)
Resurgam
For John Booth, of Ingoldmells, who m. 1805, Hannah, dau. of
Willingham Franklin, sister of Sir John Franklin, and d. 9 Oct.
1854.   (Source, as 1.)

3. All black background
Booth arms only
Crest: A lion passant argent   Mantling: Gules and
argent   Motto: In coelo quies
Unidentified

GAINSBOROUGH Old Hall
1. Dexter background black
Qly, 1st and 4th, Gules on a chief argent two molets pierced sable
(Bacon), 2nd, Barry of six argent and azure a bend gules (Quadlope),
3rd, Argent three towers gules (Towers), in centre chief the Badge of
Ulster   In pretence: Gules a fess between three boars' heads couped
or ermined sable (Beckett)
Crest: A boar passant ermine   Mantling: Gules and
argent   Motto: Mediocria firma

For Sir Henry Hickman Bacon, 10th and 11th Bt., who m. 1853,
Elizabeth, dau. of Sir Thomas Beckett, Bt., and d. 14 Nov.
1872.   (B.P. 1949 ed.)

GRAINSBY

1. Dexter background black
Azure a saltire between in pale two molets and in fess two crescents
addorsed argent (Haigh), impaling, Or on a fess sable between three
trefoils slipped azure three martlets or (Harty)
Crest: A rock proper   No mantling   Motto: Sola virtus invicta
For George Henry Haigh, who m. 1859, Emma Jane Adelaide, youngest
dau. of Sir Robert Way Harty, Bt., and d. 1887.   (B.L.G. 5th ed.;
B.P. 1875 ed.)

GRANTHAM

1. All black background
On a lozenge surmounted by a cherub's head
Ermine on a chevron azure three fountains, in chief the Badge of Ulster
(Cust)   In pretence: Or an escutcheon azure within an orle of
martlets gules (Brownlow)
Motto: In coelo quies
For Anne, dau. of Sir William Brownlow, 4th Bt., and sister and sole
heir of John, Viscount Tyrconnel, who m. 1717, Sir Richard Cust, 2nd
Bt., and d. 29 Dec. 1779.   (B.P. 1949 ed.)

2. Dexter background black
Or two bars azure a chief qly azure and gules, on first and fourth two
fleurs-de-lys or, on second and third a lion passant guardant or
(Manners), impaling, Qly, 1st and 4th, Or a fret azure (Tollemache),
2nd and 3rd, Azure a crown or between three molets argent (Murray)
Crest: A peacock in his pride proper   Mantling: Gules and
argent   Motto: Pour y parvenir
For John Manners of Hanby Hall, who m. 1765, Louisa, Countess of
Dysart, and d. 23 Sept. 1792.   (B.P. 1949 ed., Dysart)
(There is another hatchment for John Manners at Bottesford, Leics)

3. All black background
Per pale azure and gules three lions rampant or, the Badge of Ulster
(   ), impaling, Manners, all within a bordure compony ermine and
sable ermined argent, on a canton or a saltire gules
Cherub's head above
Unidentified

4. Dexter background black
Per chevron argent and sable in chief two moorcocks sable
(Middlemore), impaling, Argent a human heart gules imperially
crowned proper, on a chief azure three molets argent (Douglas)

Crest: A moorcock azure   Mantling: Gules and argent   Motto:
indecipherable
For William Richard Middlemore, of Somerby Hall, who m. Mary, dau.
and co-heir of James Douglas, M.D. of Carlisle, and d. 7 Mar. 1772,
aged 42.   (M.I.; Lincs Peds.)

5. All black background
Middlemore, impaling, Azure a fess between three molets or (   )
No crest   Mantling: Gules and argent   Motto: indecipherable
Unidentified

6. Dexter background black
Qly, 1st, Per bend sinister or ermined sable and azure a lion rampant or
(for Penant), 2nd, Azure three birds between two bars or a chief or
(   ), 3rd, Azure three boars in pale or (Philip Phichdon), 4th, Or on
a bend azure three fleurs-de-lys or (Gruffyd Lloyd)
Crest: From a ducal coronet or a ram's head proper   Mantling:
Gules and argent   Motto: indecipherable   Skull and crossbones
below
Unidentified

LITTLE GRIMSBY
1. All black background
Argent on a pale sable a sword erect argent hilted or (Nelthorpe)
Crest: Out of clouds proper an arm fesswise proper holding a sword
erect argent hilted or   No mantling   Motto: Mors janua
vitae   Skull and crossbones below
Possibly for John Nelthorpe, of Little Grimsby Hall, who d.
1784.   (Lincs Peds.)

2. All black background
Arms: As 1.
Crest: As 1.   Mantle: Gules and ermine   Motto: Resurgam
Possibly for John Nelthorpe, of Little Grimsby Hall, who d.s.p.
1737.   (Source, as 1.)

HACKTHORN
1. All black background
Azure on a bend indented argent three martlets sable (Cracroft),
impaling, Qly, 1st and 4th, Argent a cross Calvary gules, on a chief
azure four roundels argent (Weston), 2nd and 3rd, Argent three bars
azure surmounted by three pallets gules, on a chief or a lion passant
azure (Patrick)
Crest: A stork holding a battleaxe proper   Mantling: Gules and
argent   Motto: Resurgam

For John Cracroft, who m. 1782, Penelope Anne, dau. of the Rev. Dr. Charles Fleetwood Weston, of Somerby Hall, and d. 2 Oct. 1821.   (B.L.G. 5th ed.; Lincs Peds.)

2. Dexter background black
Argent a tower triple-towered between three covered cups azure (Amcotts)
No helm   Crest: A squirrel sejant gules collared or in the forepaws a nut proper   Mantle: Gules and ermine   Loyaul en service
For Weston Cracroft Amcotts, who d. 14 July 1883.   (B.L.G. 1937 ed.)

HARLAXTON
1. Dexter background black
Gules on a chevron between ten cross crosslets or three cross crosslets gules (Gregory), impaling, Qly of six, 1st and 6th, Gules a lion rampant or (   ), 2nd, Argent a rose gules (   ), 3rd, Gules a chevron argent between three ?goats' heads erased or (   ), 4th, Argent a griffin segreant within a bordure gules (   ), 5th, Gules a chevron argent between three human heads couped at the shoulders proper (   )
Crest: Three garbs or   Mantling: Gules and argent   Motto: Resurgam   Skull above crest
Probably for George Gregory, of Harlaxton Manor, who m. Susana, dau. and heir of William Williams, of Rempstone, Notts, and d. 10 Apr. 1746.   (Lincs Peds.)

2. Dexter background black
Two coats per fess, in chief, Gregory with a canton or, and in base, Argent on a bend engrailed azure between two stags' heads cabossed proper an eagle's head erased between two escallops or (Longden), both impaling, Sable a fess between two chevrons ermine (Holden)
Crests: Dexter, Three garbs or   Sinister, An eagle wings displayed in its dexter claw a stag's head cabossed proper   Mantling: Gules and argent   Motto: Resurgam
For John Sherwin-Gregory, of Harlaxton Manor, and Bramcote Hills, who m. Catherine, dau. of Robert Holden, of Nuttall Temple, and d. 1869.   (B.L.G. 7th ed.)
(There is another hatchment for John Sherwin-Gregory at Bramcote, Notts)

HORBLING
1. All black background
Argent two lions passant sable in chief a molet gules for difference (Brown), impaling, Per fess nebuly or and azure three martlets counterchanged (Barker)

Crest: An eagle's head sable between two wings azure beaked
or   Mantling: Gules and argent   Motto: Resurgam
For Edward Brown of Walcot, who m. Sarah, dau. of Thomas Barker,
and d. 6 May 1841, aged 92.   (B.E.B.; Lincs Peds)

HORKSTOW
1. All black background
Qly, 1st and 4th, Paly of six or and azure a canton ermine (Shirley),
2nd and 3rd, qly i. & iv. France, ii. & iii. England
Crest: A Saracen's head couped proper wreathed at the temples or and
azure   Mantling: Gules and or   Motto: Semper paratus
For Admiral Thomas Shirley, who m. 2nd, Anne, dau. of Thomas Hele,
and d.s.p. 7 Apr. 1814.   (B.P. 1963 ed.; M.I.)

2. All black background
On a lozenge   Two coats per fess, in chief, Shirley, and in base,
Azure on a fess argent between three ostrich feathers erect proper three
martlets sable (Tufnell), impaling, Gules a bend fusilly ermine (Hele)
Motto: Resurgam
For Anne, dau. of Thomas Hele, who m. 1st, Admiral Thomas Shirley,
and 2nd, Colonel John Tufnell, and d.   (B.P. 1963 ed.)

3. Dexter background black
Tufnell, impaling, Hele
Crests: Dexter, A dexter arm in armour proper holding a cutlass
argent   Sinister, On a chapeau gules and ermine an falcon rising
proper   Mantling: Gules and or   Motto: Resurgam
For Colonel John Tufnell, who m. Anne, dau. of Thomas Hele, and
widow of Admiral Thomas Shirley, and d. 18 Mar. 1838.   (G.M.)

HORNCASTLE
1. All black background
Paly of six or and sable, on a chief gules a lion passant or (Lodington),
impaling, Gules three escallops within a bordure engrailed or (Earle)
Motto: Mors iter ad vitam
For the Rev. Thomas Lodington, Vicar, 1678-1724, who m. 2nd, 1708,
Prudence Earle, and d. 21 Mar. 1724.   (M.I.)

2. All black background
On a lozenge   Sable two lions passant guardant in pale argent
ducally crowned or (Dymoke)   In pretence: Azure a lion rampant
or (Snowden)
For Jane, only dau. of Robert Snowden, who m. Charles Dymoke, of
Scrivelsby, Champion of England, and d. 4 Jan. 1743.   (M.I.)

HUMBERSTON

1. Dexter background black

Argent three bars or ermined sable in chief three roundels sable
(Humberston), impaling, Sable three chevrons ermine (Wyse)
Crest: On a chapeau gules and ermine a griffin's head erased argent
charged with three roundels in pale sable   Mantling (very full):
Gules and argent   Motto: Moriendo vivo
For Matthew Humberston, who m. 2nd, Mary, dau. of John Wyse, of
London, and d.s.p. 28 Aug. 1709.   (Harl. Soc., Vol. 51, p. 522)

IRNHAM

1. All black background

Per pale or and azure two chevronels engrailed between three
cinquefoils counterchanged, a crescent for difference (Woodhouse),
impaling, Argent a bull passant gules a bordure sable bezanty (Cole)
Crest: A demi-griffin azure semy of cinquefoils or in the dexter claw an
arrow point downwards argent   Mantling: Gules and
argent   Motto: Virtus in arduis
For William Hervey Woodhouse, who m. Sarah Ellen Cole, and d. 16
May 1859.   (M.I.)

LANGTON-BY-SPILSBY

1. Dexter background black

Qly of six, 1st, Qly sable and or a bend argent (Langton), 2nd, Or fretty
azure on a canton gules a cross moline or (Mumby), 3rd, Sable four
martlets rising argent (Mewter), 4th, Argent three palmers' staves sable
(Palmer), 5th, Or a chevron gules (   ), 6th, Argent a fess gules
between three garbs sable (Tindall), impaling, Sable ermined argent on
a cross quarter-pierced argent four millrinds sable (Turnor)
Crest: An eagle or and a wyvern vert erect and interwoven
Mantling: Gules and argent   Motto: In coelo quies
For George Langton, who m. 1736, Diana, dau. of Edmund Turnor of
Stoke Rochford, and d. 1769, aged 73.   (B.L.G. 1937 ed.)

2. Dexter background black to both shield and lozenge

An oval shield and a lozenge   Shield, Qly of six, as 1., impaling,
Gules a lion rampant argent (Lloyd), with crest, as 1.
above   Lozenge, surmounted by a countess's coronet, Qly, 1st and
4th, Argent on a bend azure three buckles or (Leslie), 2nd and 3rd, Or a
lion rampant gules debruised by a bendlet sable (Abernethy), impaling,
Lloyd
Supporters (to lozenge): Two griffins per fess argent and
gules   Cherubs' heads above and below
For Bennet Langton, who m. 1770, Mary, Dowager Countess of Rothes,
dau. of Gresham Lloyd, and d. 1801, aged 64.   (B.L.G. 1937 ed.)

3. Dexter background black

Argent a cross moline gules (Uvedale), impaling, Per chevron azure and argent in chief two eagles rising or (Stephens)
Crest: From a chapeau gules and ermine two feathers, the dexter argent the sinister gules   Mantling (very full): Gules and argent   Motto: Tant que je puis
For Robert Uvedale, the horticulturist, who m. Mary, 2nd dau. of Edward Stephens of Charington, and d. 17 Aug. 1722.   (D.N.B.)

MAREHAM-ON-THE-HILL

1. All black background

On a lozenge surmounted by a cherub's head
Azure a cross flory or (Ward)   In pretence: Qly, 1st and 4th, Sable three pheons argent (Nicolls), 2nd and 3rd, Vert on a cross wavy or an· estoile vert (Adams)
In an ornamental gilt frame
Probably for Mary, dau. of the Rev. Samuel Nicolls, by Rose Adams, who m. the Rev. Richard Ward, and. d. post 1814.   (Lincs Peds.)

MARSTON

1. All black background

Or a chevron gules between three roundels sable, on a chief azure a cock between two cross crosslets fitchy or (Lucas), impaling, Sable three goats salient argent (Thorold)
A skull and crossbones in each corner   A small hatchment, *c.* 2 ft. by 2 ft., on wood panel
For George Lucas, of Fenton, who m. Penelope, dau. of Sir William Thorold, 1st Bt., and d. 31 Jan. 1690. She d. 1658.   (B.P. 1949 ed.; H. Thorold)

2. Dexter Background black

Qly, 1st, Sable three goats salient argent, in chief the Badge of Ulster (Thorold), 2nd, Argent three bars gules, on a canton azure a martlet or (Hough), 3rd, Argent a cross potent gules between four roundels sable (Brerehaugh), 4th, Argent a bend raguly between six roundels sable (Marston)
Crest: A stag trippant ermine attired or   Mantling: Gules and argent   Willow branches in base
For Sir John Thorold, 4th Bt., who m. 1701, Margaret Waterer, widow of the Hon. Francis Coventry, and d.s.p. 14 Jan 1716/17.   (B.P. 1949 ed.)

3. All black background

On a lozenge   Sable three goats salient argent (Thorold)
On a wood panel *c.* 2 ft. by 2 ft.
For Dorothy Frances, widow of the Rev. Ernest Hayford Thorold, Chaplain-General, d. 14 Mar. 1969.   (B.P.)

MOULTON

1. Sinister background black

Sable three birdbolts fesswise proper armed and feathered argent
(Boulton), impaling, Sable a bend or on a canton argent a leopard's face
gules (Isaac)
Mantling: Gules and argent   Motto: Spes mea in Deo   Escallop
above shield
For Harriet, dau. of the Rev. Baptist Isaac, of Dorset, who m. as his 3rd
wife, Henry Boulton, and d. 3 Mar. 1806.   (Monson's Church
Notes)

2. Sinister background black

Boulton, as 1.   In pretence: Azure a lion rampant sable ermined or
crowned or (Durell)
Mantling: Gules and argent   Motto: Spes mea in
Deo   Cherub's head above
For Mary, dau. of Lt.-Colonel Durell, who m. as his 4th wife, Henry
Boulton, and d. 9 Apr. 1808.   (Source, as 1.)

3. Dexter background black

Azure three birdbolts fesswise or (Boulton), impaling, Qly, 1st and 4th,
Qly azure and gules three crescents between three saltires or (Lane),
2nd, Or a bend vair cotised gules (Bowyer), 3rd, Gules a bezant between
three demi-lions or (Bennet)
Crest: A tun or banded gules   Mantling: Gules and or, with two
gold tassels   Motto: Requiescat in pace
There are also four small shields one in each corner of
hatchment   In chief, Boulton, with in pretence, Argent a chevron
between three buglehorns vert stringed or a crescent for difference
(Forster)   Dexter, Boulton, impaling, Qly, 1st and 4th, Argent a
bend gules between two lions' heads erased sable (Francklin), 2nd and
3rd, Sable on a chevron azure between three bugles or three pheons or
(Forster)   Sinister, Boulton impaling Isaac   In base, Boulton,
with Durell in pretence   Black background to all four small shields
For Henry Boulton, who m. 1st, Susanna, eldest dau. and co-heiress of
Mr. Serjeant Forster, d. 5 Sept. 1788. He m. 2nd, Mary, dau. of John
Francklin, of co. Bedford, d. 4 Sept. 1795. He m. 3rd, Harriet, dau. of
the Rev. Baptist Isaac, of Dorset, d. 3 Mar. 1806. He m. 4th, Mary
Winifreda, dau. of Lt.-Colonel Durell, d. 9 Apr. 1808. He m. 5th, and
lastly, Emma, 4th dau. of Thomas Lane, of Selsdon, Surrey, and d. 11
Mar. 1828.   (M.I.)

NEWTON-ON-TRENT

1. Dexter background black

Azure a cross between four leopards' heads cabossed or (Stow),
impaling, Gules a chevron argent between three herons argent
(Armstrong)

Knight's helm   Crest: A leopard's face between two wings erect
or   Mantling: Gules and argent   Motto: Pax aeterna . . .
For John Stowe, of Newton, who m. Mary, dau. of the Rev. Andrew
Armstrong, and d. 1744.   (Lincs Peds. Vol. III)
(This hatchment is very faded, and the blazon is taken largely from
Monson's Church Notes)

NORTON DISNEY

1. All black background
Argent a bear rampant sable muzzled or (   ), impaling, Per chief
gules and sable a lion rampant or (   )
No helm, crest, mantling or motto   Skull in base   A small
hatchment on a wood panel
Unidentified

REDBOURNE

1. Sinister background black
Qly, 1st and 4th, qly i. & iv. France and England qly, ii. Scotland, iii.
Ireland, over all a baton sinister gules charged with three roses argent
(Beauclerk), 2nd and 3rd, Qly gules and or in the first quarter a molet
or (Vere), impaling, Qly, 1st and 4th, Argent on a pale sable a sword
erect argent pommel and hilt or (Nelthorpe), 2nd and 3rd, Sable on a
bend dancetty argent three martlets sable (Cracroft)
Duchess's coronet   Mantle: Gules and ermine   Supporters:
Dexter, An antelope argent armed and unguled or   Sinister, A
greyhound argent   Each gorged with a collar gules charged with
three roses argent
For Maria Janetta, only dau. of John Nelthorpe, of Little Grimsby Hall,
who m. as his 2nd wife, William, 8th Duke of St Albans, and d. 17 Jan.
1822.   (B.P. 1949 ed.)

2. All black background
Arms: As 1.
Duke's coronet   Crest: On a chapeau gules and ermine a lion
statant guardant or ducally crowned per pale argent and gules and
gorged with a collar gules charged with three roses argent   Mantle
and supporters: As 1.   Motto: Auspicium melioris aevi
For William, 8th Duke of St Albans, who d. 17 July 1825.   (B.P.
1949 ed.)

3. Sinister background black
Qly, 1st and 4th, Beauclerk, 2nd, Vere, 3rd, Or three chevronels gules a
label of three points azure (   )   In pretence: Azure on a fess
between three pheons argent two buckles gules (for Mellon)
Duchess's coronet   Mantle and supporters: As 1.

For Harriet, dau. of Matthew Mellon, who m. 1827, as his 1st wife,
William Aubrey de Vere, 9th Duke of St Albans, and d. 6 Aug.
1837.   (B.P. 1949 ed.)

4. All black background

Qly, as 3., impaling, Ermine a griffin segreant gules between three
crescents or (for Gubbins)
Duke's coronet   Crest, motto and supporters: As 2.
For William Aubrey de Vere, 9th Duke of St Albans, who m. 2nd, 1839,
Elizabeth Catherine, youngest dau. of Gen. Joseph Gubbins, of Kilfrush,
co. Limerick, and d. 27 May 1849.   (B.P. 1949 ed.)
(These four hatchments are now in the Usher Art Gallery, Lincoln)

RIBY

1. Sinister background black

Qly, 1st and 4th, Gules a lion passant between three molets or
(Pretyman), 2nd and 3rd, Argent a chevron azure between three oak
leaves vert (Tomline)   In pretence: Argent a fess between three
crescents (Amler)
Motto: Resurgam   Three cherubs' heads above and skull below
For Frances, only child of John Amler, of Ford Hall, Salop, who m.
1811, William Edward Tomline, of Riby Grove, and d. 30 Apr.
1816.   (B.L.G. 1937 ed.)

2. All black background

Arms: As 1.
Crests: Dexter, Two lions gambs erased argent holding a molet
or   Sinister, On a mural coronet a martlet argent   Mantling:
Gules and argent   Motto: Resurgam
For William Edward Tomline, who d. 28 May 1836.   (B.L.G. 1937
ed.)

3. All black background

Tomline arms only
Crest: not discernible   Mantling and motto: As 2.   Skull below
Probably for Marmaduke Tomline of Riby, who d. unm. 22 June
1803.   (Lincs Peds.)

SAXBY

1. Dexter background black

Argent a fess gules between three popinjays vert beaked and clawed
gules (Lumley), impaling, Qly, 1st and 4th, Or fretty azure
(Willoughby), 2nd and 3rd, Or on two bars gules three water bougets
two and one argent (Willoughby)
Earl's coronet   Crest: A pelican in her piety proper   Mantle:
Gules and ermine   Motto: Murus aeneus conscientia
sana   Supporters: Two parrots vert beaked and clawed gules

For Richard, 6th Earl of Scarbrough, who m. 1787, Henrietta (d. Mar. 1846), dau. of Henry, 5th Baron Middleton, and d.s.p. 17 June 1832.   (B.P. 1949 ed.)

2. All black background

Qly, 1st and 4th, Argent on a bend sable three owls argent (Savile), 2nd and 3rd, Lumley
Earl's coronet   Crests: Dexter, An owl argent   Sinister, As 1., with motto above as 1.   Motto below shield: Bee
fast   Supporters: As 1.
Probably for John, 8th Earl of Scarbrough, who d. unm. 29 Oct. 1856.   (B.P. 1949 ed.)

SCAWBY

1. All black background

Argent on a pale sable a sword erect argent pommel and hilt or, the Badge of Ulster (Nelthorpe)
Crest: Out of clouds a hand and arm fesswise holding a sword proper   Mantling: Gules and argent   Motto:
Resurgam   Skull in base
Probably for Sir Henry Nelthorpe, 7th Bt., who d.s.p. 12 May 1830.   (B.P. 1855 ed.)

2. Dexter background black

Nelthorpe, with Badge of Ulster, impaling, Argent a chevron between three crosses flory sable (Anderson)
Crest: As 1.   Motto: Fortitudine
For Sir John Nelthorpe, 8th Bt., who m. 1838, Frances Maria, dau. of the Rev. Sir Charles Anderson, Bt., and d. 22 Nov. 1865.   (B.L.G. 1937 ed.; B.P. 1855 ed.)

3. Identical to 2., but much smaller and with the background all black   No frame
Probably also for Sir John Nelthorpe, and perhaps used subsequently by his widow, who d.   (Source, as 2.)

4. Sinister background black

Argent a canton sable (Sutton), impaling, Nelthorpe   Crossed palm branches below
For Charlotte, only sister of Sir John Nelthorpe, 8th and last Bt., who m. 1847, the Rev. Robert Sutton, and d. 11 Nov. 1872.   (B.L.G. 1937 ed.)

SCOTTON

1. All black background

Qly of six, 1st and 6th, Or on a chief azure three doves argent
(Frederick), 2nd, Argent three moorcocks proper (?Marisco), 3rd, Argent
a lion rampant between two molets in fess gules a chief ermine
(Moncrieff), 4th, Per pale or and vert and per chevron embattled three
martlets all counterchanged (Hudson), 5th, Or two lions passant
between three cross crosslets sable (Garth)
Crest: On a chapeau azure and ermine a dove argent   Motto:
Resurgam
For the Rev. Christopher Frederick, Rector of Scotton, 1810-63, some
time chaplain to George IV when Prince of Wales, d. unm. Sept.
1863.   (B.P. 1875 ed.)

SPALDING

1. All black background

Sable a chevron between three cross crosslets fitchy argent
(Buckworth)   In pretence: Per pale azure and sable a lion rampant
between three escallops argent (Clay)
Crest: A lion rampant argent holding in dexter paw a cross crosslet
fitchy argent   Mantling: Gules and argent   Motto: In coelo
quies
For Theophilus Buckworth, of Clay Hall, Spalding, who m. Elizabeth
Clay, and d. 3 Feb. 1802. She d. 3 Jan. 1793.   (Church Notes)

2. Sinister background black

Or a water bouget sable, on a chief sable three annulets or (Johnson),
impaling, Sable a chevron between three cross crosslets fitchy argent
(Buckworth)
Motto: Mors janua vitae   Two cherubs' heads above
For Ann Elizabeth, dau. of Theophilus Buckworth, who m. the Rev.
Maurice Johnson, Rector of Spalding, and. d. 3 Jan. 1827.   (B.L.G.
2nd ed.; M.I.)

3. All black background

Johnson, impaling, Qly, 1st and 4th, Buckworth, 2nd and 3rd, Azure a
lion rampant between three annulets argent (Clay)
Crest: From a ducal coronet or two wings erect sable   Mantling:
Gules and argent   Motto: Onus sub honore
For the Rev. Maurice Johnson, who d. 25 May 1834.   (Sources, as
2.)

4. Sinister background black

Qly, 1st and 4th, Johnson, 2nd and 3rd, Argent a chevron sable between
three lions' heads erased gules (Johnson of Pinchbeck)   In pretence:
Per fess argent and sable a pale counterchanged three bears salient sable
(Mills)

Motto: Resurgam   Knot of blue ribbons above shield and
medallions within wreaths flanking it
For Elizabeth, only dau. and heir of the Rev. Thomas Mills, Canon of
Peterborough, who m. 1841, as his 1st wife, Maurice Johnson, of
Ayscough Fee Hall, and d. 25 Sept. 1843.   (B.L.G. 5th ed.)

5. Dexter background black
Johnson, impaling, Azure a chevron ermine between three swans argent
(Swan)
Crest and mantling: As 3.   Motto: Spes coelo
For Maurice Johnson, who m. 2nd, Isabella Mary Susan, dau. of
J. Swan, of Lincoln, and d. 8 Oct. 1864.   (B.L.G. 5th ed.)

6. Dexter background black
Johnson, impaling, Argent a chevron between three moorcocks sable
(Moore)
Crest, mantling and motto: As 3.
For Theophilus Fairfax Johnson, who m. Millicent Anne, dau. and sole
heir of Stephen Roger Moore, and d. 29 Mar. 1853.   (B.L.G. 5th
ed.)

7. All black background
On a lozenge   Qly, 1st, Per fess sable and or in chief two annulets
or in base a water bouget sable (Johnson), 2nd, Argent three pallets
wavy gules (Downes), 3rd, Argent a chevron gules between three lions'
heads erased proper ducally crowned or (Johnson of Pinchbeck), 4th,
Sable a cross ermine in dexter chief a leopard's face argent
(Ambler)   In pretence: Moore, with chevron engrailed
For Millicent Anne, widow of Theophilus Fairfax Johnson, d.
          (B.L.G. 5th ed.)

8. Sinister background black
Johnson, as 2., impaling, Gules two bars gemel between three escallops
or (Rigge)
Crest, mantling and motto: As 3.
For Caroline, dau. of Gray Rigge, of Wood Broughton, Lancs, who m.
1850, Theophilus Maurice Stephen Johnson, and d. 16 July
1871.   (B.L.G. 5th ed.; M.I. in Weston St Mary)

9. All black background
Qly of 18, 1st, Johnson, as 2., 2nd, Vert three lions rampant argent
(Tyson), 3rd, Gules a cross patonce or (De Vesci), 4th, Or on a cross
sable an escallop or (Fitzjohn), 5th, Gules three water bougets argent
(Redhead), 6th, Gules three fleurs-de-lys argent between two bendlets
barry or and azure (Atkirke), 7th, Or two bars azure in chief a martin
sable (St Martin), 8th, Argent three pallets wavy gules (Downes), 9th,
Or a chevron between three lions' heads erased gules (Johnson of

Pinchbeck), 10th, Azure three stags trippant or (Green), 11th, Argent a
fess between three bugles stringed gules (Ogle), 12th, Or on a bend
sable a bezant (Pinchbeck), 13th, Or an orle sable (Bertram), 14th,
Sable a cross ermine in dexter chief a leopard's face or (Ambler), 15th,
Argent on a bend azure three crosses formy or (Sybsey), 16th, Qly or
and gules on a bend azure three roses argent seeded or (Lessington),
17th, Azure an estoile or between three crescents argent (Thorpe), 18th,
Argent a chevron engrailed between three moorcocks argent
(Moore)   To dexter of main shield, Johnson, impaling, Rigge
S.B1.   To sinister of main shield, Johnson, impaling, Chequy or and
gules on a chevron sable three roses or (Vaux) D.B1.
Crests: Dexter, From a ducal coronet or two wings erect
argent   Sinister, A lion's head erased gules ducally crowned
between two feathers argent   Motto: Requiescat in pace
For Theophilus Maurice Stephen Johnson, who d. 11 Dec.
1892.   (Sources, as 8.)

STOKE ROCHFORD
1. All black background
Qly, 1st, Sable ermined argent on a cross quarter-pierced argent four
millrinds sable (Turnor), 2nd, Argent on a chevron sable three gouttes
or (Erneys), 3rd, Barry of six argent and sable six escutcheons three, two
and one argent each charged with a lion rampant sable, in chief a
crescent gules for difference (Cecil), 4th, Per bend indented argent and
gules two lions' heads erased counterchanged crowned or (Ferne),
impaling, Argent on a fess gules three fleurs-de-lys or (Disney)
Crest: A lion passant argent gorged or in its dexter paw a millrind
sable   Mantling: Gules and argent   Motto:
Resurgam   Skull below
For Edmund Turnor, who m. Mary, dau. of John Disney, of Lincoln,
and d. 22 Jan. 1805, aged 89.   (B.L.G. 1937 ed.)

2. Dexter two-thirds background black
Qly, 1st, Turnor, 2nd, Erneys, 3rd, Argent a fess and in chief a lion
passant guardant sable (   ), 4th, Azure a bend embattled or
(   ), impaling to dexter, Or a cross engrailed per pale gules and
sable (Broke), and to sinister, Azure a chevron between three sea-horses
argent (Tucker)
Crest and mantling: As 1.   Motto: In coelo quies
For Edmund Turnor, who m. 1st, 1795, Elizabeth (d. 1801), dau. of
Philip Broke, and 2nd, Dorothea (d. 1854), dau. of Lt.-Colonel Tucker,
and d. 19 Mar. 1829.   (B.L.G. 1937 ed.; M.I.)

3. Dexter background black
Gules in chief two helmets proper barred or in base a garb or, the Badge
of Ulster (Cholmeley), impaling, Qly, 1st and 4th, France and England

qly, 2nd, Scotland, 3rd, Ireland, over all a baton sinister gules charged
with three roses argent (Beauclerk)
Crests: Dexter, A demi-griffin proper, beaked, winged and clawed or, in
its claws a helmet proper barred or   Sinister, An eagle's head erased
or   Mantling: Gules and argent   Motto: Resurgum
For Sir Montagu John Cholmeley, 2nd Bt., who m. 1829, Georgiana, 5th
dau. of William, 8th Duke of St Albans, and d. 18 Jan. 1874.   (B.P.
1949 ed.)

SURFLEET
1. Dexter background black
Qly, 1st and 4th, Sable a chevron between three cross crosslets fitchy
argent (Buckworth), 2nd, Gules a fess nebuly between three estoiles
argent (Everard), 3rd, Ermine on a canton azure a pelican or (Pell?),
impaling, Azure a chevron ermine cotised between three martlets or
(Northon)
Crest: A demi-lion in its paws a cross crosslet fitchy
argent   Mantling: Gules and argent   Motto: Spes mea in Deo
For Theophilus Buckworth, who m. Ann, dau. of John Northon, of
Holbeach, and d. 17 Feb. 1801, aged 63.   (M.I.)

SWINHOPE
1. Dexter background black
Sable a bend engrailed between six billets argent (Alington), impaling,
Gules a doubleheaded eagle displayed or, on a chief or three estoiles
gules (Atkinson)
Crest: A talbot passant argent   Motto: Non pour haine   On a
wood panel
For the Rev. Marmaduke Alington, who m. Anne, dau. of the Rev. John
Emeris of Louth, whose mother was an Atkinson heiress, and d. 3 Aug.
1840.   (B.L.G. 1937 ed.; M.I.)

TEALBY
1. Dexter background black
Qly of 16, 1st, qly i. & iv. Azure a fess dancetty between ten billets four
and six or (D'Eyncourt), ii. & iii. Gules three leopards' faces or jessant-
de-lys azure over all a bend azure (Tennyson), 2nd, Tennyson, 3rd,
Argent a cross engrailed between four roundels sable (Clayton), 4th,
Indecipherable, 5th, Argent two bars azure (Hilton), 6th, Gules nine
popinjays or (Twenge), 7th, Or a saltire gules on a chief gules a molet
or (Bruce), 8th, Gules two arches proper (Arches), 9th, Or a saltire
gules (Neville), 10th, Argent two bars gules, on a canton gules a lion
passant guardant or (Lancaster), 11th, Sable a fess between three fleurs-
de-lys argent (Welby), 12th, Argent a saltire engrailed sable charged
with nine annulets argent (Leke), 13th, Argent three fleurs-de-lys in fess
azure between eight cross crosslets sable (Hilary), 14th, Vair a fess gules
(Marmion), 15th, Barry of six argent and azure in chief three roundels

gules (Grey), 16th, Azure three cinquefoils or (Bardolf)   In
pretence: Argent on a fess sable three stags' heads cabossed or (Hutton)
Crests: Dexter, A lion passant guardant argent ducally crowned or, the
dexter paw resting on an escutcheon of the arms of
D'Eyncourt   Sinister, A dexter arm in armour holding in the hand a
broken spear enfiled with a laurel wreath proper   Mottoes: En
avant   Nil temere
For the Rt. Hon. Charles Tennyson-D'Eyncourt, P.C., of Bayons Manor,
who m. 1808, Frances Mary, only child and heir of the Rev. John
Hutton, of Morton, Lincs, and d. 21 July 1861.   (B.L.G. 1937 ed.)
(This hatchment is damaged and in need of restoration)

THORGANBY
1. All black background
Argent two chevronels engrailed sable each charged with three bezants,
in dexter chief a crescent or for difference (Rothwell)
Crest: From a ducal coronet or a stag's head argent   Mantling:
Sable and or
Unidentified

UFFINGTON
1. Dexter background black
Vert three harts courant within a bordure argent, the Badge of Ulster
(Trollope), impaling, Argent a chevron between three garbs gules all
within a bordure compony argent and azure (Sheffield)
Baron's coronet   Motto: Audio sed taceo   Supporters: Two stags
argent attired and ducally gorged or
For John, 1st Baron Kesteven, who m. 1847, Julia Maria, eldest dau. of
Sir Robert Sheffield, 4th Bt., and d. 17 Dec. 1874.   (B.P. 1949 ed.)

2. All black background
Argent three battering rams proper headed azure (Bertie)
Earl's coronet   Crest: A Saracen's head couped at the breast proper
ducally crowned or   Mantle: Gules and ermine   Motto:
Loyauté me oblige   Supporters: Dexter, A friar vested with staff in
dexter hand proper   Sinister, A savage wreathed about the loins
with ivy proper
Probably for George Augustus Frederick Albemarle, 10th Earl of
Lindsey, who d. unm. 21 Mar. 1877.   (B.P. 1949 ed.)

UTTERBY
1. All black background
Argent on a cross gules five bells argent (Sedgewick), impaling, Argent
a fess engrailed azure between six fleurs-de-lys sable, a crescent for
difference (Eley)
Crest: blacked out   Mantling: Ermine
A small hatchment, *c.* 2 ft. by 2 ft.

For the Rev. Thomas Sedgwick, who m. 1697, Elizabeth Ely, and
d.   (Lincs Peds.)

WELL
1. All pale blue background
Ermine on a chief indented vert three eagles' heads erased or, a crescent
for difference, the Badge of Ulster (Chaplin), impaling, Sable a fret
argent (Harington)
Crest: An eagle's head erased or murally gorged vert   Mantling:
Gules and argent   On motto scroll: Sr Robt Chaplin Bt   A
very small hatchment, *c.* 18 in. by 18 in., on wood panel in ornate frame
For Sir Robert Chaplin, 1st Bt., who m. Ann, dau. of John Harrington,
of Kelston, and d. 1 July 1728.   (B.P. 1949 ed.; Lincs Peds. I, 236)

2. Sinister background black
Qly, 1st and 4th, Or on a fess sable between three ducks proper a rose
or (Bateman), 2nd and 3rd, Argent on a fess between three crescents
gules three fleurs-de-lys or (Oakeley)   In pretence: Ermine on a
chief indented vert three eagles' heads erased or (Chaplin)
On motto scroll: Mrs. Ann Bateman, obit 7 Mar 1732/3   A very
small hatchment, *c.* 20 in. by 20 in., in ornate frame
For Anne, only dau. and heir of Sir Robert Chaplin, 1st Bt., who m. the
Hon. James Bateman, and d. 7 Mar. 1732/3.   (Inscr. on hatchment/
B.P. 1949 ed.)

3. All black background
Arms: As 2.
Crest: A demi-Muscovy duck rising proper collared
argent   Mantling: Gules and argent   Motto: Mors janua
vitae   Winged skull below   A very small hatchment, *c.* 20 in.
by 20 in., in ornate frame
For the Hon. James Bateman, who d.   (B.P. 1949 ed.)

4. Dexter background black
Argent on a fess cotised gules three griffins' heads erased or
(Dashwood)   In pretence: Qly, 1st and 4th, Bateman, 2nd, Ermine
on a chief gules three eagles' heads erased or (Chaplin), 3rd, Argent on
a fess between three crescents sable three fleurs-de-lys or (Oakeley)
Crest: A griffin's head erased per fess or and gules   Mantling: Gules
and argent   Motto: Mors janua vitae   A very small hatchment,
c. 20 in. by 20 in.
For Samuel Dashwood, who m. 1743, Ann, dau. and heiress of James
Bateman, of Well Vale, and d. Dec. 1792.   (M.S. Ped. Dashwood
family)

5. All black background
Identical to 4.

Although not on lozenge, presumably for Ann, widow of Samuel
Dashwood. She d. 15 May 1802.   (Source, as 4.)

WILSTHORPE
1. Dexter background black
Two cartouches   Dexter, Sable a fess cotised between three martlets
or (Smith)   In pretence: Paly of six or and azure a fess chequy or
and azure (Curtis)   Sinister, Azure a griffin segreant or
(Morland)   Crest: not discernible   Mantling: Gules and
argent   Motto: Semper fidelis
For Sir John Smith, 1st Bt., High Sheriff of Dorset 1772, who m. 1st,
Elizabeth (d. 13 Feb. 1796), dau. and heiress of Robert Curtis, of
Wilsthorpe, and 2nd, Anna Eleanora, eldest dau. of Thomas Morland,
of Court Lodge, Kent, and d. 13 Nov. 1807.   (B.P. 1949 ed.)
(There was until recently also a hatchment for Sir John at Sydling St
Nicholas, Dorset)

NOTTINGHAMSHIRE

by

K. Train, F.S.A.

Tuxford 1: For Sir Thomas Woollaston White, 1st Baronet, 1817
(*Photograph by The National Monuments Record*)

INTRODUCTION

In 1959 the Nottinghamshire Local History Council pro-
moted a survey of the existing hatchments in Nottinghamshire,
but the actual recording was done by the staff of the City
Library. This was supervised by Mr. F. C. Tighe, the late
City Librarian, Miss V. W. Walker was responsible for the
heraldic descriptions and identification and Mr. G. L. Roberts
photographed them and deposited the transparencies in the
Central Library, Nottingham. Miss Walker published descriptions of the hatchments in the *Transactions of the Thoroton
Society for 1965*, Vol. LXIX.,

I have looked at all these hatchments, carefully checked
the blazons and descriptions, correcting them where necessary;
several other examples have been added.

There are now 75 hatchments in 25 churches and one in
the Castle Museum, Nottingham, once in Markham Clinton
church. The hatchment of George Gordon Noel, 6th Lord
Byron, the poet, is included though it does not resemble an
orthodox hatchment, being set in a square frame.

It has not been possible to identify all the hatchments, but
the earliest appears to be that to Mrs. Joan Mellish, 1708, at
Blyth, and there are many more 18th-century examples. Except for four of the 20th century the rest belong to the 19th
century. A hatchment at Tuxford, used as the frontispiece, has
28 quarterings, the largest number found in the county. The
most recent one is at Car Colston to Thomas Colston Blagg,
who died on 13 October 1983.

One example from the previous list is not included here; it
is for Mrs. Grace Fanshawe at Kelham, who died in 1763, but
it appears to be an integral part of her monument. Although
the earliest typical hatchment is for Mrs. Joan Mellish, at
Blyth, the much earlier example for William Cressy in St
Peter's, Nottingham, has been included, for although it bears
an inscription we cannot be certain that it was intended as a
permanent memorial.

Since the survey took place more interest has been taken in the hatchments of the county and more than twenty have been well restored, particularly those at Flintham, Gedling and Oxton.

Keith Train, F.S.A.

Since the death of Keith Train in March 1985, it has been necessary to update his original draft to take in slight alterations and additions. This I have been pleased to do.

W. F. Webster
23 Roseleigh Ave,
Mapperley
Nottingham

ATTENBOROUGH

1. Dexter background black

Two oval shields   Dexter, within circlet of the Order of the Bath, and with badge pendent below, Qly, 1st and 4th, Chequy or and azure, on a canton gules a lion rampant argent (Warren), 2nd and 3rd, Argent on a bend sable two arms emerging from clouds proper rending a horseshoe or (Borlase), over all the Badge of Ulster   Sinister, arms as dexter, impaling, Qly or and gules a bend sable (Clavering) Crests: Dexter, From a ducal coronet or a plume of feathers argent   Sinister, A wolf passant reguardant argent in its mouth an arrow or which pierces its shoulder   Mantling: Gules and argent   Motto: Leo de Juda est robur nostrum   Supporters: Two wyverns argent armed and winged gules each holding a banner chequy or and azure
For Admiral Sir John Borlase Warren, Bt., G.C.B., who m. Caroline, dau. of General Sir John Clavering, K.C.B., and d. 27 Feb. 1822.   (B.E.B.; Complete Baronetage)

2. Dexter background black

Azure on a chevron or between three swans argent three cinquefoils gules (Charlton), impaling, Chequy or and gules a lion rampant ermine, on a canton azure a castle triple-towered argent (Scarlett)
Crest: A swan's head and neck erased argent beaked gules gorged with a chaplet vert   Mantling: Azure and or   Motto: Stabit conscius aequi   Inscribed below motto: Nicholas John Charlton   Charlie
For Nicholas John Charlton, who m. 2nd, 1885, Helen Scarlett, dau. of William, 3rd Lord Abinger, and d. 1892.   (B.L.G. 1937 ed.)

AVERHAM

1. Sinister background black

Ermine on a chief indented azure three griffins' heads erased or (Chaplin), impaling, Argent a canton sable (Sutton)
Mantling: Gules and argent   Motto: As God will   Cherub's head above
For Anne Georgiana, dau. of Sir Richard Sutton, 1st Bt., who m. 1796, the Rev. Robert Chaplin, rector of Averham, and was bur. 25 Mar. 1826, aged 52.   (P.R.: B.P. 1949 ed.)

2. All black background

Arms: As 1.

Crest: A griffin's head erased or murally gorged vert   Mantling and
motto: As 1.
For the Rev. Robert Chaplin, rector of Averham, who d. 30 May
1837.   (B.P. 1949 ed.; G.M. 1837, ii, 210)

BEESTON
1. All black background
Qly, 1st and 4th, Azure on a bend gules three garbs or (Rickards), 2nd
and 3rd, Gules a chevron or between three wedges argent each bearing
four trefoils slipped sable (   )
Crest: Out of the battlements of a tower proper a demi-talbot azure
langued and collared gules   Mantling: Azure and
argent   Motto: Esto quod esse videris
Probably for John Rickards, who d. 2 Aug. 1821, aged 75.   (M.I. in
church)

BLYTH
1. All black background
On a lozenge surmounted by a cherub's head
Sable three lions rampant argent (Prowse), impaling to dexter, Or a
chevron between three leopards' faces gules (Harvey), and to sinister,
Azure two swans in pale argent between three claunches ermine, in fess
point a molet argent for difference (Mellish)
Cherub's head below
For Joan, dau. and co-heiress of Thomas Prowze, of Willesden, Devon,
who m. 1st Tobias Harvey, of Womersley, and 2nd, Samuel Mellish,
and d. Jan. 1708/9. He d. 23 Oct. 1707.   (Trans. of Thoroton
Society, 1908, Vol. 5; History and Antiquities of the Parish of Blyth,
1860)

2. Dexter background black
Azure two swans in pale argent between two flaunches ermine (Mellish),
impaling, Gules a fess between three cross crosslets fitchy or (Gore)
Crest: A swan's head and neck erased argent ducally gorged
or   Mantling: Gules and argent
For Joseph Mellish, who m. Dorothea, dau. of Sir William Gore, Lord
Mayor of London, and d. June 1733, aged 58.   (Sources, as 1.; P.R.)

3. Dexter background black
Mellish   In pretence and impaling, Sable a chevron ermine between
three herons close argent (Herne)
Crest and mantling: As 2.
For Edward Mellish, who m. 1741, Sarah Herne, and d. 2 Jan. 1757,
aged 49.   (Sources, as 1., M.I.)

4. Dexter background black
Mellish, impaling, Argent a lion rampant sable (Stapleton)

Crest and mantling: As 2.   Motto: Resurgam
For Charles Mellish, Recorder of Newark, who m. Judith Stapleton, and
d. Jan. 1797.   (Sources, as 1.)

5. All black background
On a lozenge   Arms: As 4.
Motto: In coelo quies
For Judith, widow of Charles Mellish, d. 1806.   (Sources, as 1.)

6. Dexter background black
Mellish   In pretence: Qly, 1st and 4th, Gules three lions passant
guardant in pale or (for Giffard), 2nd, Per fess argent and azure three
chaplets proper (Duke), 3rd, Per pale embattled gules and argent
(   )
Crest and mantling: As 2.   Motto: In coelo quies
For Colonel Henry Francis Mellish, who m. Harriet, dau. of Sir Duke
Giffard, Bt., of Castle Jordan, Ireland, and d. July 1817.   (Sources,
as 2.)

7. All black background
Qly, 1st and 4th, Mellish, 2nd and 3rd, Gules a cross engrailed argent,
in the dexter chief quarter an escutcheon argent charged with two bars
azure, over all a bend compony argent and gules (Leigh), impaling,
Azure on a fess wavy cotised wavy argent three anchors sable (Cunard)
Crest and mantling: As 2.
For Colonel William Leigh Mellish, who m. Margaret Ann, dau. of Sir
Samuel Cunard, and d. 18 Apr. 1864.   (Sources, as 1.)

8. All black background
On a lozenge   Argent a chevron fimbriated sable between three
chamber pieces fired proper (Chambers), impaling, Mellish
For Anne, dau. of Charles Mellish, who m. 1811, William Cecil
Chambers, and d. 12 Aug. 1855, aged 74.   (Sources, as 1.)

9. All black background
On a lozenge   Arms: As 2.
For Dorothea, widow of Joseph Mellish, d. Jan. 1737, aged
54.   (Sources, as 2.)
(This hatchment was recorded after the National Survey began in 1952,
but has since disappeared)

10. All black background
Mellish arms only   To dexter of main shield, Mellish, impaling,
Gules six broken bones two, two and two, the joint almost meeting in
pale argent (Da Costa) A.B1.   To sinister of main shield, Mellish
with, in pretence, Gules (Details not discernible) D.B1.

For William Mellish, who m. 1st, Catherine da Costa, widow of Villa
Real, Esq. She d. 1746. He m. 2nd, Anne, dau. and co-heir of John
Gore, and d. Dec. 1791. She d. 1794.   (Sources, as 2.)
(This hatchment was recorded in poor condition after the National
Survey began in 1952, but has since disappeared)

BRAMCOTE
1. Dexter background black
Qly, 1st and 4th, Gules on a chevron between nine cross crosslets or
three cross crosslets gules, a canton or (Gregory), 2nd and 3rd, Argent
on a bend engrailed azure between two bucks' heads cabossed proper a
griffin's head erased between two escallops or (Longden), impaling, Per
pale sable and ermine a fess between two chevrons all counterchanged
(Holden)
Crests: Dexter, Three garbs or banded gules, the centre garb charged
with a cross crosslet gules   Sinister, An eagle with wings expanded
proper, charged on the breast and on either wing with an escallop azure,
and supporting with the dexter claw a buck's head cabossed
proper   Mantling: Gules and or   Motto: Crux scutum
For John Sherwin-Gregory (né Longden), of Harlaxton Manor and
Bramcote Hills, who m. Catherine, dau. of Robert Holden, of Nuttall
Temple, Notts., and d. 7 June 1869.   (B.L.G. 5th ed.)
(There is another hatchment for John Sherwin-Gregory at Harlaxton,
Lincs)

BUNNY
1. Dexter background black
Gules on a chevron or between three stags trippant proper three boars'
heads couped azure, on a chief or a griffin passant sable (Forteath)
Crest: A stag's head erased or   Mantling: Gules and
argent   Motto: Tam animo quam mente sublimis
For George Alexander Forteath, of Bunny Hall, who d. 3 Oct.
1862.   (M.I. in church)

2. All black backgound
Qly, 1st and 4th, Argent an eagle displayed sable, on a canton or a fess
dancetty between seven billets sable ermined argent (Parkyns), 2nd and
3rd, Argent a lion rampant fork-tailed sable (Cressy), impaling two
coats per fess, in chief, On a mount vert a windmill proper (Sampson),
and in base, Argent a bear salient gules (Barnat), in fess point of shield
the Badge of Ulster
Crest: A pineapple or   Mantling: Gules and argent   Motto:
Honeste audax   Skull below
For Sir Thomas Parkyns, 2nd Bt., who m. 1st, Elizabeth, dau. of John
Sampson, of Breason, Derby, and 2nd, 1728, Jane, dau. of Mr. Alderman
Barnat, and d. 29 Mar. 1741.   (B.P. 1949 ed.)

3. Sinister background black

Qly, 1st, Parkyns with eleven billets, 2nd, Argent a bear sejant sable
(Beresford), 3rd, Cressy, 4th, Gules a fess wavy and in chief three piles
in point wavy argent (Isham), in chief the Badge of Ulster   In
pretence:Parkyns
Crest, mantling and motto: As 2.   Cherub's head above
For Jane, dau. and heir of Thomas Parkyns, of East Leake, who m. 1747,
as his 1st wife, Sir Thomas Parkyns, 3rd Bt., and d. 24 Dec.
1760.   (B.P. 1949 ed.)

CAR COLSTON

1. All black background

On a lozenge   Argent two bendlets engrailed between two pouches
sable stringed or (Blagg), impaling, Gules a lion rampant argent
crowned or (Hayward)
For Ethel Mary, 3rd dau. of William Knight Hayward, of Navenby,
Lincs, who m. Thomas Matthews Blagg, of Brunsell Hall, Car Colston,
and d. 10 Nov. 1974, aged 89.
(Hatchment painted by J. Norman Dowse, of Newark-on-Trent)

2. All black background

Blagg arms only
Crest: A pouch or blague ermine stringed or   Mantling: Sable and
argent   Mottoes: Partage votre blague, and, Resurgam
For Thomas Colston Blagg, of Brunsell Hall, who m. 1st, Loys Willis,
dau. of Frederick John Cope, and 2nd, Elizabeth Mary, dau. of Lt.-Col.
Richard Booth, and d. 13 Oct. 1983.
(Hatchment painted by J. Norman Dowse, of Newark-on-Trent)

CARLTON-IN-LINDRICK

1. All black background

Argent on a chevron between three fleurs-de-lys sable three rams' heads
couped argent (Ramsden), impaling, Sable six martlets argent, on a
chief argent three bucks' heads cabossed gules (Uppleby)
Crest: A cubit arm mailed proper the hand grasping a fleur-de-lys
sable   Mantling: Gules and argent   Motto: Resurgam
For Robert Ramsden, of Carlton Hall, who m. 1783, Elizabeth, eldest
dau. of John Uppleby, of Wootton, Lincs, and was bur. 4 May
1830.   (B.L.G. 1937 ed.; Bishop's transcript)

2. All black background

Qly, 1st and 4th, Argent on a chevron between three fleurs-de-lys sable
three rams' heads erased argent (Ramsden), 2nd and 3rd, Argent on a
bend between two unicorns' heads erased azure three lozenges or
(Smyth)
Crest and mantling: As 1.   Motto: Christo redemptus in Christo
dormio
Unidentified

ELTON

1. All black background

On a lozenge suspended from a lovers' knot

Qly, 1st and 4th, Per saltire sable and gules three molets of six points in bend argent between two bendlets dancetty or (Launder), 2nd and 3rd, Argent on a chevron engrailed azure between three martlets sable three crescents or (Watson)

Mantling: Gules and argent   Motto: In coelo quies

For Frances, dau. and co-heiress of Cornelius Launder, d. 14 Mar. 1822.   (M.I.)

2. Sinister background black

Azure a maunch argent, over all a bend gules, all within a bordure engrailed ermine (Norton)   In pretence: Qly, 1st and 4th, Launder, 2nd and 3rd, Watson

Mantling: Gules and argent   Motto: In coelo quies   Cherub's head above

For Ursula, dau. and co-heiress of Cornelius Launder, who m. as his 1st wife, William Fletcher Norton Norton, and d. 18 Jan. 1845.   (M.I.)

3. Dexter background black

Azure a maunch ermine over all a bend gules (Norton), impaling, Argent three greyhounds courant in pale sable (Briscoe)

Crest: A Moor's head affronté, couped at the shoulders proper, charged on the neck with a trefoil or, wreathed round the temples with laurel proper, with a scarf ermine over the right shoulder   Mantling: Gules and argent   Motto: Resurgam

For William Fletcher Norton Norton, who m. 2nd, Sarah Briscoe, and d. 15 Nov. 1865. (M.I.)

FLINTHAM

1. Dexter background black

Qly, 1st and 4th, Argent a fess between three buglehorns sable (Thoroton), 2nd, Argent a lion rampant per fess gules and sable (Lovetot), 3rd, qly i. Per pale indented argent and sable, ii. & iii. Argent a fleur-de-lys azure, iv. Per pale indented sable and argent (Morin), impaling, Or two bars azure a chief qly azure and gules, in the first and fourth quarters two fleurs-de-lys or, in the second and third a lion passant guardant or (Manners)

Crest: A lion rampant per fess gules and sable between the paws a buglehorn sable   Mantling: Gules and argent   Motto: Deus scutum et cornu salutis

For Thomas Thoroton, of Screveton Hall, who m. Roosilia Drake, natural daughter of John, 3rd Duke of Rutland, and d. 9 May

1794.   (B.L.G. 1937 ed.; Godfrey, Notes on the Churches of Notts, Hundred of Bingham, 1907, p. 398)
(This hatchment was formerly in the parish church at Screveton)

2. Dexter backgound black

Qly, 1st and 4th, Argent a fess between three buglehorns sable stringed gules (Thoroton), 2nd, Argent a lion rampant per fess gules and sable langued azure (Lovetot), 3rd, qly i. & iv. Per pale indented azure and argent, ii. & iii. Argent a fleur-de-lys azure (Morin)   In pretence: Argent three bows stringed palewise in fess proper between ten fusils gules (Bowes)
Crest: A lion rampant per fess gules and sable, langued azure, holding between the paws a buglehorn sable   Mantling and motto: As 1.
For Colonel Thomas Thoroton, of Screveton Hall and Flintham Hall, who m. Anne, dau. and co-heir of George Wanley Bowes, of Eyford, Glos., and Thornton Hall, co. Durham, and d. 13 Nov.
1813.   (Sources, as 1.; Hildyard family)

3. Dexter background black

Qly, 1st and 4th, Azure a chevron between three molets or (Hildyard), 2nd and 3rd, qly i. & iv. Thoroton as 1., ii. & iii. Bowes with nine fusils, impaling, Hildyard
Crest: A cock sable combed, legged and wattled gules   Mantling: Gules and argent   Motto: ΠΛΕΟΝ ΗΜΙΣΥ ΠΑΝΤΟΣ
For Colonel Thomas Blackborn Hildyard, who m. Anne Catherine Whyte, niece and heiress of Sir Robert Darcy Hildyard, 4th Bt., and d. 30 July 1830.   (Sources, as 2.)

4. Dexter background black

Qly, 1st and 4th, Azure a chevron argent between three molets or (Hildyard), 2nd and 3rd, Argent a fess between three buglehorns stringed sable (Thoroton)   In pretence: Qly, 1st and 4th, Sable an eagle displayed with two heads argent charged on the breast with an ermine spot, within a bordure engrailed argent (Hoare), 2nd and 3rd, qly i. & iv. Gules three cinquefoils ermine (Hamilton), ii. & iii. Argent a lymphad sails furled sable (Arran), in fess point over the sub-quartered coats a crescent sable; on a chief of honourable augmentation, Argent a mount vert thereon a castle, a Spanish flag flowing from the battlements all proper, beneath inscribed 'Alba de Tormes' in gold letters (Hamilton Augmentation)
Crest: A cock sable, combed, legged and wattled gules   Mantling: Gules and argent
For His Honour Judge Gerard Hildyard, Q.C., who m. 1911, Sybil, dau. of Henry William Hamilton Hoare (who assumed additional name of Hamilton in 1908), and d. 22 April 1956. (Sources, as 2.)

GEDLING

1. Sinister background black

Qly ermine and gules (Stanhope), impaling, Or on a bend azure three pheons or (Thistlethwaite)

Countess's coronet   Mantle: Gules and ermine   Motto: A Deo et rege   Supporters: Dexter, A wolf or ducally crowned gules   Sinister, A talbot ermine

For Anne, dau. of the Rev. Robert Thistlethwayte, D.D., of Norman Court and Southwick Park, Hants, who m. 1777, as his 1st wife, Philip, 5th Earl of Chesterfield, and d. 20 Oct. 1798.   (B.P. 1949 ed.)

2. Sinister background black

Two oval shields   Dexter, within the Garter, Stanhope   Sinister, Qly, 1st and 4th, Barry of ten or and sable (Boteville), 2nd and 3rd, Argent a lion rampant tail nowed and erect gules (Thynne)

Countess's coronet   Mantle and motto: As 1.   Supporters: Dexter, as 1.   Sinister, A reindeer or

For Henrietta, 3rd dau. of Thomas, 1st Marquess of Bath, K.G., who m. 1799, as his 2nd wife, Philip, 5th Earl of Chesterfield, and d. 31 May 1813.   (B.P. 1949 ed.)

3. All black background

Two oval shields   Arms: As 2.

Earl's coronet   Crest: A tower azure, thereon a demi-lion rampant or ducally crowned gules holding between the paws a grenade fired proper   Mantle: Gules and ermine   Motto (above crest and below shield): A Deo et rege   Supporters: As 2.

For Philip, 5th Earl of Chesterfield, K.G., who d. 29 Aug. 1815.   (B.P. 1949 ed.)

4. Dexter background black

Stanhope, impaling, Qly, 1st and 4th, Qly per fess indented argent and sable in the first and fourth quarters a buglehorn sable (Forester), 2nd and 3rd, Azure a fess nebuly between three crescents ermine, in centre chief a cross botonny fitchy argent for difference (Weld)

Earl's coronet   Crest: As 3.   Motto: A Deo et rege   Supporters: As 1.

For George, 6th Earl of Chesterfield, who m. 1830, Anne Elizabeth, eldest dau. of Cecil, 1st Baron Forester, and d. 1 June 1866.   (B.P. 1949 ed.)

5. Sinister background black

Per pale azure and gules three lions rampant argent a crescent argent for difference (Herbert)   In pretence: Qly ermine and gules (Stanhope)

Countess's coronet   Supportrs: Dexter, A panther guardant argent semy of roundels gules and azure, ducally gorged per pale azure and gules, flames issuing from the mouth and ears proper, chained or, charged on shoulder with ermine spot   Sinister, A lion argent ducally gorged per pale azure and gules, chained or, charged on the shoulder with an ermine spot

For Evelyn, only dau. of George, 6th Earl of Chesterfield, who m. 1861, as his 1st wife, Henry Howard Molyneux, 4th Earl of Carnarvon, and d. 25 Jan. 1875.   (B.P. 1949 ed.)

HUCKNALL TORKARD

1. All black background

On a lozenge with cherubs' head above and winged skull below

Argent three bendlets enhanced gules (Byron)   In pretence: Qly, 1st and 4th, Azure a star between three boars' heads couped sable (Gordon), 2nd and 3rd, Or a fess wavy gules (for Davidson)

For Catherine, dau. of George Gordon, of Gight, who m. 1785, as his 2nd wife, Capt. John Byron, and d. 1 Aug. 1811.   (B.P. 1949 ed.)

2. Dexter background black

Qly, 1st and 4th, Byron, 2nd and 3rd, qly i. & iv. Azure a star between three boars' heads couped close or langued gules (Gordon), ii. & iii. Azure a fess between three pheons or (Davidson)

Baron's coronet   Motto: Crede Byron

For George Gordon Noel, 6th Baron Byron, the poet, son of Capt. John Byron and Catherine Gordon (No. 1), who d. 19 Apr. 1824.   (B.P. 1949 ed.)

(This hatchment is unusual in that the wife's arms are not shown, there are no supporters or crest, and it is painted to hang square not lozengeways)

LANGFORD

1. Dexter background black

Chequy sable and argent on a bend gules three molets or (Haffenden), impaling, Argent on a chevron gules between two anvils in chief and in base an anchor proper a bee proper between two crescents argent (Walker)

Crest: An eagle's head couped proper   Mantling: Gules and argent   Motto: In coelo quies

For James Haffenden, of Tenterden, Kent, who m. 1813, Katherine, dau. of Joseph Walker, of Eastwood House, Rotherham, and d. 2 Aug. 1838, aged 51.   (M.I. in church)

NORTH MUSKHAM

1. Sinister background black

Qly, 1st, Azure a fess ermine between two lions passant or ermined sable (Dickinson), 2nd, Argent on a fess between three escutcheons gules three molets or pierced sable (Bacon), 3rd, Argent a dexter gauntlet sable (Lacock), 4th, Argent a cross engrailed gules between four molets

azure, on a chief or three damask roses gules seeded or barbed vert
(Allgood), impaling, Ermine a lion rampant sable (Kenrick)
Mantling: Gules and argent   Motto: Mors janua
vitae   Cherub's head above
For Harriet, dau. of John Kenrick, of Bletchingley, Surrey, who m.
William Dickinson, historian of Newark and Southwell, and d. 22 Nov.
1805.   (M.I.)

2. All black background
Qly, 1st, Dickinson, 2nd, Argent on a fess engrailed between three
escutcheons gules three molets or (Bacon), 3rd, Argent a dexter gauntlet
sable garnished or (Lacock), 4th, Argent a cross engrailed between four
molets gules, on a chief azure three damask roses argent seeded or
barbed vert (Allgood), impaling, Kenrick
Crest: Two arms embowed in armour proper in the hands a human heart
gules inflamed or charged with a tower tripletowered
argent   Mantling: Gules and argent   Motto: Mors janua vitae
For William Dickinson, who d. 9 Oct. 1822.   (M.I.)

NOTTINGHAM Castle Museum
1. All black background
Within the Garter, Qly, 1st and 4th, Argent six cross crosslets fitchy,
three, two, one sable, on a chief azure two molets or (Clinton), 2nd and
3rd, qly i. & iv. Azure three pelicans vulning themselves argent, ii. &
iii. Gules two pieces of belt erect in pale buckles upward argent
(Pelham), impaling, Qly, 1st and 4th, Per pale gules and sable on a
cross engrailed argent five lozenges azure, on a chief or three eagles' legs
erased azure (Mundy), 2nd and 3rd, Gules an escutcheon within an orle
of martlets argent (Chadwick)
Duke's coronet   Motto: Loyaulte n'a honte   Supporters: Two
greyhounds argent collared and lined gules
For Henry, 4th Duke of Newcastle-under-Lyme, K.G., who m. 1807,
Georgiana Elizabeth, dau. of Edward Miller Mundy, of Shipley, co.
Derby, and d. 12 Jan. 1851.   (B.P. 1949 ed.)
(This hatchment was originally in the parish church of Markham
Clinton)

NOTTINGHAM St Peter
1. All black background
Argent a lion rampant double queued sable, a molet gules for difference
(Cressy), impaling, Barry of six argent and azure on each bar of argent
three molets gules (Jessop)
Crest: From a ducal coronet or a demi-peacock wings displayed
proper   Motto (above crest): Vix ea   Mantling: Gules and
argent
Inscribed at foot: William Cressy son of Hugh Cressy one of his May's
Iudges of King's bench in Ireland was maried to Eliz: daughter of Georg

Iessop of Brancliff in the County of York, Esq. died the Ninth of March 1645.
(This hatchment has recently been restored)

OLLERTON
1. Sinister background black
Qly of six, 1st, Sable on a bend between six escallops argent an escutcheon of Augmentation, argent a lion rampant vert (Foljambe), 2nd, Azure a fess wavy argent charged with a cross formy gules in chief two estoiles or, on a chief wavy argent a cormorant proper in the beak a branch of laver vert (Jenkinson), 3rd, Argent on a bend azure three owls or (Savile), 4th, Sable a chevron between three molets pierced argent (Shuckburgh), 5th, Azure a griffin passant and a chief or (Evelyn), 6th, Argent two bars gemel and in chief three molets pierced sable (Medley), impaling, Qly of six, 1st, Gules on a bend between six cross crosslets fitchy argent the Augmentation of Flodden (Howard), 2nd, Gules three lions passant guardant in pale or a label of three points argent (Brotherton), 3rd, Chequy or and azure (Warren), 4th, Gules a lion rampant argent ducally gorged or (Mowbray), 5th, Gules three escallops argent (Dacre), 6th, Barry of six argent and azure, over all three chaplets of roses proper (Greystock)
Crest: On a chapeau gules and ermine a tiger statant ducally gorged or   Mantling: Azure and or   Motto (above crest): Soye ferme   Badge (below motto): A sprig of oakleaves and an acorn proper issuant from a crescent argent   Supporters: Dexter, An antelope qly or and sable   Sinister, A tiger argent ducally gorged or
For Louisa Blanche, eldest dau. of Frederick John Howard, of Compton Place, Sussex, who m. 1869, as his 1st wife, Cecil George Savile Foljambe (later 1st Earl of Liverpool), and d. 7 Oct. 1871.   (B.P. 1949 ed.)
(This hatchment has recently been restored)

OXTON
1. All black background
On a lozenge surmounted by a helm
Vair a chief or, over all a bend gules charged with three molets argent (Sherbrooke)   In pretence (a lozenge): Sherbrooke
Mantling: Gules and argent   Motto: Mors mihi vita   Skull and crossbones below
Probably for Margaret, dau. of Henry Sherbrooke, of Oxton, who m. Henry Porter, of Bingham (who assumed the name of Sherbrooke in 1754), and d. 22 Dec. 1799.   (B.L.G. 1937 ed.)

2. Dexter background black
Sherbrooke, impaling, Azure a chevron argent between three foxes' heads erased or (Foxcroft)

Crest: A horse's head couped argent charged with three bars
gules   Mantling: Gules and argent   Motto: Vi si non consilio
For William Sherbrooke, of Oxton, J.P., who m. 1785, Anne, only dau.
and heir of John Foxcroft, and d.s.p. 17 Nov. 1831.   (B.L.G. 1937
ed.)

3. Dexter background black

Two oval shields   Dexter, within circlet of Order of the Bath, and
with badge of Order pendent below, Qly, 1st and 4th, Sherbrooke, 2nd
and 3rd, Argent on a chevron embattled counter-embattled azure
between three roses gules stalked and leaved vert three fleurs-de-lys
argent (Coape)   Sinister, within ornamental wreath, Qly as dexter,
impaling, Gules a chevron argent between three lions' heads erased or
ermined sable crowned argent (Pyndar)
Crests: Dexter, as 2.   Sinister, A lion's head erased gules crowned
or   Supporters: Dexter, A lion gules langued azure collared or
charged with three molets gules   Sinister, A tiger reguardant azure
collared or charged with three molets gules   Motto: As 2.
For Sir John Coape Sherbrooke, G.C.B., who m. 1811, Katherine, dau.
and heir of the Rev. Reginald Pyndar, and d.s.p. 14 Feb.
1830.   (B.L.G. 1937 ed.)

4. All black background

On a lozenge   Sherbrooke   In pretence: Sherbrooke
Motto: Resurgam   Cherub's head at each side of lozenge and one
below
Possibly also for Margaret Sherbrooke, d. 22 Dec. 1799.   (See 1.)

5. All black background

Sherbrooke arms only
Crest: A horse's head couped argent maned or charged with three bars
gules   Mantling: Gules and argent   Motto: In coelo
quies   Cherub's head at each top corner of shield and skull below
Probably for Robert Sherbrooke, son of Henry Sherbrooke, of Oxton, d.
unm. 23 Aug. 1740, aged 26.   (A Patchett Martin, Life and Letters
of Viscount Sherbrooke)

PAPPLEWICK

1. All black background

On a lozenge surmounted by a cherub's head
Qly, 1st and 4th, Or a fess gules between three elephants' heads erased
sable (Fountayne), 2nd, Or three lions passant in pale sable (Carew),
3rd, qly i. & iv. Argent three lozenges conjoined in fess gules within a
bordure sable (Montagu), ii. & iii. Or an eagle displayed sable
(Monthermer)
Motto: Resurgam

For Catherine Judith Fountayne, of Papplewick Hall, who d. 3 Mar.
1824.   (B.L.G. 1846 ed.)

RAMPTON
1. Dexter background black
Argent on a chevron sable three quatrefoils or (Eyre)   In pretence:
Ermine on a bend engrailed azure cotised azure three fleurs-de-lys or
(Bury)
Crest: A leg in armour couped at the thigh qly argent and
sable   Mantling: Gules and argent   Motto: In caelo pax
For Anthony Eyre, of Grove, who m. Judith Letitia, dau. and heiress of
John Bury, of Nottingham, and d. 14 Feb. 1788.   (B.L.G. 5th ed.;
M.I. in church)

STAUNTON
1. Sinister background black
Qly, 1st and 4th, Or a lion rampant gules (Charlton), 2nd, Gules ten
bezants, four, three, two, one (Zouch), 3rd, Argent two chevrons sable
(Staunton)   In pretence: Qly, 1st and 4th, Sable a chevron ermine
between three saltires argent (Greenwood), 2nd and 3rd, Vert a griffin
segreant and in chief three escallops or (Dand)
Motto: Sans varier
Shield suspended from a lover's knot, with a cherub's head at each top
corner and winged skull below
For Mary, youngest dau. of Dr. Greenwood, of Northampton, who m.
1725, Job Staunton Charlton, of Staunton, and. d. Mar.
1777.   (B.L.G. 1937 ed.; G. W. Staunton and F. M. Staunton, The
Family of Staunton, of Staunton, 1911)

2. All black background
Arms: As 1.
Crest: A fox's face gules   Mantling: Gules and argent   Motto:
As 1.   Skull and crossbones below
For Job Staunton Charlton, who d. Feb. 1778.   (Sources, as 1.)

3. All black background
On a fanciful lozenge suspended from a true lover's knot
Qly, 1st and 4th, qly i. & iv. Charlton, ii. & iii. Zouch, 2nd and 3rd,
Greenwood
Motto: In caelo quies
Probably for Emma, dau. of Job Staunton Charlton, d. Jan.
1797.   (Sources, as 1)

4. Identical to 3.
Probably for Anne, dau. of Job Staunton Charlton, d. 11 Apr.
1807.   (Sources, as 1.)

5. Sinister background black
Argent two chevrons sable, on a canton azure a quatrefoil or
(Staunton)   In pretence: Staunton, but without canton
Mantling: Gules and argent   Motto: Resurgam   Cherub's head
above
Probably for Elizabeth, dau. of Job Brough, who m. the Rev. John
Aspenshaw and d. 13 Apr. 1833. He d. 1851. Anne Charlton left the
Staunton estate to Elizabeth on condition that she and her husband
changed their name and took the arms of Staunton.   (Sources, as 1.)

SUTTON-IN-ASHFIELD
1. All black background
Qly, 1st and 4th, Azure a molet between three fleurs-de-lys and a
bordure engrailed argent (Unwin), 2nd and 3rd, Argent three roundels
azure each charged with a cross or (Heathcote)
Crest: A fleur-de-lys argent   Mantling: Azure and
argent   Motto: Probitas verus honos
Probably for Edward, 4th son of Samuel Unwin and Elizabeth Anne
Heathcote, d. unm. 3 May 1841.   (A. Stapleton, Notts. Occasional
Papers, 44, 1911)

TEVERSAL
1. Sinister background black
Sable a cross moline or quarter-pierced azure in centre chief the Badge
of Ulster (Molyneux), impaling, Or a fess between three wolves' heads
couped sable langued gules (Howe)
Mantling: Or and argent   Motto: En droit devant
For Diana, dau. of John Howe, of Langar Castle, who m. Sir Francis
Molyneux, 4th Bt., and d. 8 Jan. 1718, aged 59.   (B.E.B.; Complete
Baronetage)

2. All black background
Arms: As 1., but, azure a cross moline quarterpierced or
Crest: On a chapeau gules and ermine a plume of peacock's feathers
proper   Mantling: Gules and argent   Motto: En droit devant
For Sir Francis Molyneux, 4th Bt., who d. 12 Mar. 1742, aged
87.   (B.E.B.)

3. All black background
Qly of six, 1st, Sable a cross moline or quarter-pierced azure
(Molyneux), 2nd, Sable on a bend engrailed or three buglehorns sable
stringed sable (Greenhalgh), 3rd, Barry of ten argent and gules in chief
a label of five points sable (Barry), 4th, Argent a chevron between three
pelicans sable (Cranmer), 5th, Argent five fusils conjoined in fess gules
each charged with an escallop or (   ), 6th, Argent a chevron
between three molets pierced sable (   ), in fess point the Badge of
Ulster

Crest and mantling: As 2.
Possibly for Sir Charles Molyneux, 5th Bt., who d. unm. 28 July 1764,
or for Sir Francis Molyneux, 7th Bt., who d. unm. 9 June
1812).   (Sources, as 1.)

4. Dexter background black

Azure a cross flory quarter-pierced or, in dexter chief the Badge of Ulster
(Molyneux)   In pretence: Argent a chevron engrailed azure between
three roses gules barbed and seeded vert (?Challand)
Crest and mantling: As 2.   Motto: Mors mihi vita   Skull and
crossbones below
Probably for Sir William Molyneux, 6th Bt., who m. Anne, dau. and
heir of William Challand, of Wellow, Notts, and d. May
1781.   (Sources, as 1.)

5. All black background

On a fanciful shield instead of a lozenge
Azure a cross moline quarter-pierced or, in dexter chief the Badge of
Ulster (Molyneux)   In pretence (on a lozenge): As 4.
Crest, mantling and motto: As 4.   Skull and crossbones below
For Anne, widow of Sir William Molyneux, 6th Bt., d.   (Sources,
as 1.)

6. All black background

Sable a cross moline or quarter pierced azure, in dexter chief the Badge
of Ulster (Molyneux)
Crest, mantling and motto: As 2.
For possible identification see 3.

7. All black background

Azure a cross moline quarter-pierced or, in dexter chief the Badge of
Ulster (Molyneux)
Crest and mantling: As 2.   Motto: Resurgam
For possible identification, see 3.

8. All black background

On a lozenge   Per pale azure and gules three lions rampant argent,
a crescent argent for difference (Herbert), impaling, Qly, 1st and 4th,
Azure a cross moline or (Molyneux), 2nd and 3rd, Gules on a bend
between six cross crosslets fitchy argent the Augmentation of Flodden,
but without tressure (Howard)
Countess's coronet   Supporters: Dexter a panther guardant argent
semy of roundels gules and azure, charged on the shoulder with an
ermine spot, flames issuing from the mouth and ears proper, ducally
gorged per pale gules and azure and chained or   Sinister, A lion
argent charged on the shoulder with an ermine spot ducally gorged per
pale azure and gules and chained or

For Henrietta Anna, eldest dau. of Lord Henry Thomas Molyneux
Howard, who m. 1830, Henry John George, 3rd Earl of Carnarvon, and
d. 26 May 1876.   (B.P. 1949 ed.)
(The hatchment of the 3rd Earl of Carnarvon is at Burghclere, Hants)

THORNEY
1. Dexter two-thirds black
Qly, 1st and 4th, Gules a saltire argent (Nevile), 2nd and 3rd, Or fretty
gules, on a canton per pale ermine and or a galley with sails furled
sable (Nevill), impaling, two coats per pale, 1. Gules a maunch between
nine cinquefoils argent (Acklam) 2. Qly, 1st and 4th, Sable on a fess or
three maidens' heads veiled proper (Swainston), 2nd and 3rd, Sable two
lions passant paly of ten argent and gules, a canton argent
(Strangeways)
Crests: Dexter, Out of a ducal coronet or a bull's head pied
proper   Sinister, On a chapeau gules and ermine a galley with sails
furled sable   Mantling: Gules and argent   Motto: Ne vile
For Christopher Nevile, who m. 1st, 1797, Ann Elizabeth, dau. of
Jonathan Acklom, of Wiseton, and 2nd, 1815, Mary Elizabeth, dau. of
Allen Swainston, M.D., of York, and d. 10 Sept. 1844.   (B.L.G.
1937 ed.)

2. All black background, except lower half of sinister third
Qly, as 1., impaling three coats to the sinister, 1. Qly, 1st and 4th,
Argent four bars azure, on a canton or a chough proper (Hotham), 2nd
and 3rd, Gules a sword in bend proper hilted or (Gee) 2. & 3. per fess,
in chief argent, and in base sable, presumably for Wright and Tooth
Crests, mantling and motto: As 1.
For the Rev. Christopher Nevile, Vicar of Thorney, who m. 1st,
Gertrude, dau. of Lt.-Col. George Hotham, and 2nd, Margaret, dau. of
John Wright, and 3rd, Mary Ann, dau. of Robert Tooth, and d. 8 Aug.
1877.   (B.L.G. 1937 ed.)

TOLLERTON
1. Dexter background black
Two coats per fess, in chief, Gules two bars gemel argent, on a chief
argent five trefoils azure (Pendock), in base, Gules three bars embattled
argent (Barry), impaling, Argent a fess gules between two bars gemel
wavy azure (Eliot)
Crest: On the top of a tower gules a demi-pelican with wings endorsed
vulning herself proper   Mantling: Gules and argent   Motto:
Pro prole semper
For Pendock Neale, who m. Harriet, dau. of Richard Eliot, of Port Eliot,
Cornwall, and d.s.p. Nov. 1772.   (B.L.G. 2nd ed. & Godfrey, Notes
on the Churches of Nottinghamshire, Hundred of Bingham, p. 464)

2. Dexter background black

Qly, 1st and 4th, Gules two bars gemel and a chief argent (Pendock),
2nd, Argent three bars embattled gules (Barry), 3rd, Argent three bars
gules (Barry), impaling, Azure a hart statant argent (Lowe)
For the Rev. John Neale, Rector of Tollerton, who m. Elizabeth, dau. of
John Lowe, of Denby, Derbyshire, and d. 13 May 1781.   (Sources,
as 1.; S. P. Potter, A History of Tollerton, 1929)

3. All black background

On a lozenge surmounted by an escallop
Two coats per fess, in chief, Gules two bars argent (Pendock), in base,
Argent two bars embattled gules (Barry), impaling, Lowe
For Elizabeth, widow of the Rev. John Neale, d. 2 Mar.
1795.   (Sources, as 2.)
(A very small hatchment, *c.* 2 ft. by 2 ft.)

4. Sinister background black

Qly, 1st and 4th, Argent a fess gules between in chief two crescents and
in base a buglehorn sable (Neale), 2nd, Gules two bars gemel argent,
on a chief argent five trefoils azure (Pendock), 3rd, Argent three bars
embattled gules (Barry), impaling, Qly, as dexter, with a crescent for
difference
Motto: Mors janua vitae   Cherub's head above shield
For Susanna, dau. of the Rev. Thomas Neale, of Thimbleby, Lincs, who
m. her cousin, Pendock Neale (who later assumed the surname of
Barry), and d. 22 Apr. 1811.   (Sources, as 2.)

5. All dark red background

Qly, 1st and 4th, Gules three bars embattled argent (Barry), 2nd, Barry
of six gules and argent, on a chief argent five trefoils azure (Pendock),
3rd, Argent a fess gules between in chief two crescents and in base a
buglehorn stringed sable (Neale)
Crests: Dexter, On a mount vert a stag or charged with three lozenges in
fess argent (Neale)   Centre, The top of a tower gules charged below
the battlements with three roses in fess argent (Barry)   Sinister,
Pendock, as 1.   Motto: A rege et victoria   Supporters: Two lions
rampant guardant argent murally gorged gules, chained or, each
holding a banner with the arms of Barry
Probably for Pendock Barry (formerly Neale, and husband of 4.), who d.
13 Mar. 1833.   (Sources, as 2.)

6. All black background

Gules three bars embattled argent (Barry)
Crests: Dexter, On a mount vert a stag argent charged with the lozenges
in fess azure   Centre, The top of a tower gules charged below the
battlements with a fess argent on which are three roses
gules   Sinister, Pendock as 1.
Motto: As 5.   Supporters: As 5, but chained gules   Skull below

Possibly for Pendock Barry Barry, son of Pendrock Barry, d. 3 July
1847.   (Sources, as 2.)

7. Dexter background black
Qly, 1st and 4th, Pendock, as 1., 2nd and 3rd, Gules three bars
embattled argent (Barry), impaling, Argent on a bend sable three
pheons or, in sinister chief a crescent gules for difference (Bland)
Crest and mantling: As 1.   Motto: Mors janua vitae   Cherub's
head below
For John Neale of Tollerton, who m. 1745, Jane Bland of
Mansfield.   (Notts. Mar. Lics.)

8. All black background
On a lozenge   Qly, 1st and 4th, Sable a goat argent standing on a
child proper, swaddled gules banded argent, feeding on a tree vert
(Davies), 2nd, Or a pheon sable (   ), 3rd, Argent a saltire sable, on
a chief or three lions rampant gules (Cupper)
For Mrs. Susannah Davies, who d. 3 Nov. 1872.   (M.I. in
churchyard)

TUXFORD
1. All black background
Qly of 28, 1st and 28th, Gules a chevron vair between three lions
rampant or, the Badge of Ulster (White), 2nd, Argent on a chevron
gules between three anchors azure three escallops or (Taylor), 3rd,
Gules three arms in armour embowed in pale proper (Armstrong), 4th,
Qly ermine and or three molets pierced sable (Wollaston), 5th, Argent a
cross raguly gules, on a chief gules a lion passant guardant or
(Lawrence), 6th, Or three pallets sable, on a chief gules three horses'
heads or (March), 7th, Argent three bars and in chief three roundels
sable (Humberston), 8th, Argent three bars gules in chief a hound
courant sable (Skipwith), 9th, Qly sable and argent a bend or
(Langton), 10th, Argent three bars azure, on each bar three cross
crosslets or (Menithorpe), 11th, Azure a lion rampant ermine
(Fitzsymon), 12th, Azure three crescents argent (Thorpe), 13th, Argent
on a cross engrailed sable five mascles or (Arches), 14th, Argent a cross
lozengy gules (Flinton), 15th, Argent a cross engrailed gules (De la
Lynde), 16th, Lozengy gules and or a canton ermine (Neville), 17th, Or
two lions passant guardant gules (Fitzgerald), 18th, Argent three eagles
displayed gules (Courcy), 19th, Gules a lion rampant argent
(Meschines), 20th, Barry of ten or and gules (Rumelli), 21st, Sable three
chessrooks and a chief or (Ormesby), 22nd, Qly ermine and chequy or
and azure (Gibthorpe), 23rd, Or a chevron gules between three fleurs-de-
lys azure (Hiltoft), 24th, Or fretty azure, on a canton gules a cross flory
argent (Moneby), 25th, Sable on a hand or a falcon argent (More), 26th,
Gules a chevron between nine cross crosslets or (Kime), 27th, Vert a
saltire engrailed or (Hawley), impaling, Gules a bend embattled or

ermined sable cotised argent between two garbs or, on a chief per pale argent and or a knife azure handle or (?Blagg)
Crest: From a ducal coronet argent a demi-eagle rising
sable   Mantling: Gules and argent   Motto: Loyal until death
For Sir Thomas Woollaston White, 1st Bt., who m. 1801, Elizabeth, dau. of Thomas Blagg, and d. 28 Oct. 1817.   (B.P. 1949 ed.)

2. All black background

Arms: As dexter of 1., except for 13th quarter, which is, Argent a cross engrailed sable
Crest, mantling and motto: As 1.
For Sir Thomas Woollaston White, 3rd Bt., who d. unm. 20 May 1907.   (B.P. 1949 ed.)
Painted by Mr. J. Norman Dowse of Nottingham.

STAFFORDSHIRE

by

John E. Titterton

Weston-under-Lizard: For Selina, Countess of Bradford, 1894
(*Photograph by Mr. D. C. Mee*)

INTRODUCTION

The work for this county should be credited to the late Mr. Joe Tindale who recorded the majority of Staffordshire hatchments. Mr. Tindale was an assiduous helper in recording hatchments not only for Staffordshire but for most counties of England and Wales.

There are 57 hatchments recorded for the county. Nearly one third of these can be accounted for at two churches. At Sandon there are seven for the Barons/Earls of Harrowby and date from 1803 with two for the 3rd and 4th Earls who both died in 1900. This can be considered the largest authentic collection in the county because although there are ten at Mavesyn Ridware for successive generations of the Chadwick family, four are considered 19th-century productions for 17th-century ancestors.

The oldest hatchment in the county is that of Sir John Bowyer Bt. d. 1691 at Biddulph. There are only three from the 18th century; Charles Chadwick d. 1765, at Mavesyn Ridware, Francis Eld d. 1760 at Seighford and Stanford Wolferstan d. 1772 at Statfold.

There are no prime ministers or great admirals among the ranks. However there are hatchments for a Rear Admiral at Whitmore, the 2nd Duke of Sutherland at Trentham, and at Tamworth Castle for the 4th Marquess Townshend with 16 quarterings.

Four hatchments can no longer be traced which is perhaps few compared with other counties. They were at Shugborough Hall, Walsall Library and Wolseley Hall, Rugeley, now demolished.

The work of Lt.-Col. Ian Swinnerton, who has checked the blazons and indentifications of all the hatchments, is greatly appreciated.

John E. Titterton, 1987
7 Cecil Aldin Drive
Tilehurst, Reading, Berks.

ADBASTON

1. Dexter background black
Two oval shields, the dexter overlapping the sinister   Dexter, within the Order of the Bath, and cross pendent below, Qly, 1st and 4th, Argent a bend azure in chief a garb gules (Whitworth), 2nd and 3rd, Argent a cross azure between four choughs proper (Aylmer), over all the Badge of Ulster   Sinister, Qly as dexter, impaling, Gules three trumpets fesswise in pale or (Call)
Baron's coronet   Crests: Dexter, from a ducal coronet or a garb gules, with motto above, Dum spiro spero   Sinister, from a ducal coronet or a chough rising proper   Motto: Steady   Supporters: Dexter, A sailor holding a cross staff proper   Sinister, A sailor holding a leadline proper
For Matthew, 5th Baron Aylmer, who m. 1801, Louisa Anne, 2nd dau. of Sir John Call, Bt., and d.s.p. 23 Feb. 1850.   (B.P. 1963 ed.)

ASHLEY

1. Dexter background black
Per pale azure and sable a lion rampant argent holding a cross crosslet fitchy or between eight cross crosslets or (Kinnersley)
Crest: A greyhound sejant ermine under a tree proper resting his dexter paw on a cross crosslet or   Mantling: Azure and argent   Motto: Timor omnis abesto
Probably for Thomas Kinnersley, who m. 1778, Mary (d. 30 June 1825), only child at Edward Shepherd, of Sheffield, and d. 3 Nov. 1819.   (B.L.G. 5th ed.; M.I.)

2. All black background
Kinnersley, with a label of three points gules for difference
Crest, mantling and motto: As 1.
Probably for William Shepherd Kinnersley, eldest son of Thomas Kinnersley who d.s.p. 8 July 1823.   (B.L.G. 5th ed.)

3. Dexter background black
Kinnersley, impaling two coats per fess, in chief, Gules a fleur-de-lys or a chief ermine (Dixon), and in base, Azure a fess dancetty ermine between six cross crosslets fitchy or (Barnston)
No mantling   Motto: As 1.
For Thomas Kinnersley, who m. 1st, Anna, youngest dau. of Col. Dixon, of Allerton Grange, and 2nd, Mary, dau. of Roger Barnston, of Chester, and d.s.p. 4 Feb. 1855.   (B.L.G. 5th ed.)

149

4. All black background
On a lozenge surmounted by a skull and with skull below
Kinnersley arms only
Motto: As 1.
For either Elizabeth or Sarah, unmarried daughters of Thomas
Kinnersley (No. 1.)   (Harl. Soc. Vol. 38)

5. All black background
Qly, 1st and 4th, Ermine a fess gules (Ingram), 2nd and 3rd, Chequy
azure and argent (Meynell)
Crests: Dexter, A cock or combed and wattled gules   Sinister, A
horse's head erased argent   Mantling: Gules and argent   Motto:
Resurgam
For Hugo Charles Meynell-Ingram, of Temple Newsam, Yorks, and
Hoar Cross Hall, Staffs, who m. 1819, Georgiana, dau. of Frederick
Pigou, of London, and d. 25 Feb. 1869.   (B.L.G. 5th ed.; portrait
with identical arms in vestry)

ASTON-BY-STONE
1. All black background
Sable a chevron ermine between three martlets or (Jervis), impaling,
Gules a chevron between three leopards' faces or (Parker)
Viscount's coronet   Crest: Out of a naval crown or a demi-pegasus
argent winged azure charged on the wing with a fleur-de-lys
or   Motto: Thus   Supporters: Dexter, An eagle proper wings
elevated and endorsed holding a bundle of thunderbolts
proper   Sinister, A pegasus argent winged azure charged with a
fleur-de-lys or
For Edward, 2nd Viscount St Vincent, who m. 2nd, Mary Anne (d. 3
Jan. 1855), dau. of Thomas Parker, of Park Hall. co. Stafford, and d. 25
Sept. 1859.   (B.P. 1963 ed.)

AUDLEY
1. Dexter background black
Azure a lion rampant ermine holding a cross formy fitchy between eight
cross crosslets or (Kinnersley)
Crest: A greyhound sejant ermine holding a cross crosslet or under a tree
proper   Mantling: Azure and argent   Motto: Timor omnis
abesto
Unidentified

BETLEY
1. All black background
Azure two bars engrailed or charged with three boars' heads couped
erect two and one sable, in chief a crescent on a crescent for difference
(Twemlow), impaling, Sable a cross wavy or ermined sable between

four roundels argent each charged with an arrow in bend sable
(Fletcher)
Crest: A parrot sable beaked and legged gules perched on the stump of
an oak tree proper   Mantling: Gules and argent   Motto:
Fideliter
For Francis Twemlow, of Betley Court, who m. 1814, Elizabeth, dau. of
Sir Thomas Fletcher, 1st Bt., and d. 10 Mar. 1865.   (B.L.G. 1937
ed.)

BIDDULPH

1. All black background

Argent a lion rampant between three cross crosslets fitchy gules, in
dexter chief the Badge of Ulster (Bowyer), impaling, Qly, 1st and 4th,
Azure three molets argent within a tressure flory-counterflory or
(Murray), 2nd and 3rd, Or two bars sable each charged with two
escallops or (Bayning)
Peer's helm   Crest: On a tower gules a demi-dragon
or   Mantling: Gules and argent ending on each side with a tassel
below a Stafford knot   In base the date 1689   To dexter and
sinister of shield two crests, each on a mantle gules and
argent   Dexter, A mermaid proper   Sinister, An ostrich argent
holding a gold key in its beak
On a wood panel, *c.* 3 ft. by 3 ft.
For Sir John Bowyer, Bt., who m. Jane, dau. and co-heir of Henry
Murray, by Anne, Viscountess Bayning of Foxley, and was bur. 18 July
1691.   (Complete Baronetage)

BURNTWOOD

1. Dexter background black

Argent three tridents sable (Worthington), impaling, Paly of six or and
sable a bend counterchanged (Calvert)
Crest: A goat passant argent   Mantling: Sable and
argent   Motto: Virtute dignus avorum
For William Worthington, of Burton, who m. 1824, Mary Anne, 2nd
dau. of Francis Calvert, of Houndhill, and . 17 Oct. 1871.   (B.L.G.
1937 ed.)

BURTON-ON-TRENT

1. Dexter background black

Argent three sheaves of as many arrows proper banded gules, on a chief
azure a bee volant or (Peel), impaling, Peel
Crest: A demi-lion rampant argent collared azure, the collar charged
with three bezants, holding between the paws a shuttle
or   Mantling: Gules and argent   Motto: In coelo quies
For Robert John Peel, who m. 1818, Dorothy, dau. of Jonathan Peel of
Accrington House, and d. 1857.   (B.L.G. 5th ed.)

CHRISTCHURCH-ON-NEEDWOOD
1. Dexter background black
Qly, 1st, Argent a scythe the handle in bend sinister sable in fess a fleur-de-lys sable, a crescent for difference (Sneyd), 2nd, Azure a cross engrailed ermine (Stoughton), 3rd, Argent a lion rampant between three cross crosslets fitchy gules (Bowyer), 4th, Or a chevron chequy gules and azure between three cinquefoils azure (Cooke)   In pretence: Per bend azure and gules an eagle displayed or (Greaves)
Crest: A lion passant sable   Mantling: Gules and argent   Motto: Surgere mea spes est
For Edward Sneyd, of Berkeley Lodge, who m. Marie, dau. of Joseph Greaves of Mayfield, Stafford, and d. 17 Apr. 1832.   (B.L.G. 5th ed.)

2. All black background
On a lozenge   Qly, 1st and 4th, Argent a scythe the handle in bend sinister sable, on a crescent gules a label argent for difference (Sneyd), 2nd, Cooke, 3rd, Bowyer   In pretence (on a lozenge): Per bend vert and gules an eagle displayed or (Greaves)
For Marie, widow of Edward Sneyd, who d. 25 May 1848.   (Source, as 1.; M.I.)

3. Dexter background black
Azure a fess between three bucks' heads cabossed or (Barton), impaling, Qly, 1st and 4th, Argent a chevron between three molets sable (   ), 2nd and 3rd, Or on a fess between three martlets sable three crescents or (   )
Crest: An acorn leaved proper   Mantling: Azure and or   Motto: Resurgam
Unidentified

ENVILLE
1. Dexter background black
Qly, 1st and 4th, Barry of six argent and azure (Grey), 2nd and 3rd, Argent three boars' heads couped erect sable (Booth)
Earl's coronet   Crest: A unicorn passant ermine, armed, maned, tufted and unguled or, in front of a sun in splendour proper   Motto: A ma puissance   Supporters: Two unicorns ermine, armed, maned, tufted and unguled or
Probably for George Harry, 5th Earl of Stamford and 1st Earl of Warrington, who m. 1763, Henrietta (d. 4 June 1827), dau. of William, 2nd Duke of Portland, and d. 28 May 1819.   (B.P. 1949 ed.)
(There are further hatchments for the 5th Earl at Bowdon, Cheshire and Groby, Leics.)

FORTON
1. Dexter background black
Qly, 1st an 8th, qly i. & iv. Sable a cross wavy or ermined sable
between four roundels argent each charged with an arrow in bend sable
(Fletcher), ii. & iii. Argent three stags' heads cabossed sable (Boughey),
over all the Badge of Ulster, 2nd, Ermine a cross voided between four
fleurs-de-lys sable (Fenton), 3rd, Sable three molets in bend between
two bendlents or (   ), 4th, Gules a fess argent between three stags'
heads cabossed or (   ), 5th, Argent a stag's head cabossed sable
(   ), 6th, Gules three ?falchions fesswise in pale argent (   ), 7th,
Sable ten bezants, four, three, two and one, on a chief argent a lion
passant sable (Bridgman), impaling, Qly argent and gules four crosses
formy counterchanged (Chetwode)
Crests: Dexter, A roundel argent charged with a pheon per pale ermine
and sable   Sinister, From a dual coronet or a stag's head sable
collared and attired or   Mantling: Gules and argent   Motto:
Nec quaerere nec spurnere honorem
For Sir John Fenton Boughey, 2nd Bt., who m. Dorothy, dau. of Sir John
Chetwode, and d. 1823.   (B.P. 1875 ed.)

2. Dexter background black
Qly, 1st and 4th, Argent on a fess between three crescents gules three
fleurs-de-lys or, in chief of 1st quarter a crescent gules for difference
(Oakeley), 2nd and 3rd, Azure a stag trippant or (Strahan), over all the
Badge of Ulster, impaling, Gules a chevron between three spearheads
argent (Beatson)
Crests: Dexter, An arm in armour embowed the hand proper grasping a
scimitar argent hilted or   Sinister, A stag's head erased
or   Mantling: Gules and argent   Motto: Non timeo sed caveo
For Sir Charles Oakeley, 1st Bt., who m. 1777, Helena, only dau. of
Robert Beatson, of Kilrie, co. Fife, and d. 7 Sept. 1826.   (B.P. 1963
ed.)

LICHFIELD Cathedral
1. All black background
On a cartouche   Qly, 1st and 4th, Gules a cross or between twelve
cross crosslets or (Woodhouse), 2nd, Argent a lion rampant sable
charged on the shoulder with a martlet or (Mompesson), 3rd, Or an
anchor in pale sable (Chapple)   In pretence: Or ten billets, four,
three, two and one gules (for Peate)
Crest: On a coronet or a mount vert surmounted by a cross crosslet
fitchy or   No helm or mantling   Motto: In hoc
vincam   Palm branches flanking shield and winged skull below
For the Very Rev. John Chappel Woodhouse, D.D., Dean of Lichfield,
who m. Mercy Peate (d. 1826), and d. 17 Nov. 1833.   (Burke's
Commoners, iii., 614)

MAVESYN RIDWARE

1. Dexter background black

Gules an inescutcheon within an orle of martlets argent (Chadwick), impaling, Sable a handbow between two pheons argent (Cawarden) Crest: A lily stalked and leaved proper   Mantling: Gules and argent   Motto: Volate ad astra   The hatchment bears the initials I.C. and the date 1623.   On the frame of the hatchment are painted eight shields: 1. Vairy gules and argent (   ), 2. Argent a chevron gules between three martlets sable (Bagot), 3. Argent a chevron between three escallops sable (   ), 4. Vairy argent and sable (   ), 5. Gules three bendlets argent (Malveysin), 6. Sable three gauntlets azure (   ), 7. Qly gules and or in the first quarter a lion or (Massey), 8. as 5.
For John Chadwick, who m. Joyce, dau. and co-heiress of Thomas Cawarden, and was bur. 8 Aug. 1623.   (Church guide; Commoners, iii., 438; P.R.)

2. All black background

Chadwick   In pretence: Qly, 1st and 4th, Argent a chevron gules between three martlets sable, a crescent gules for difference (Bagot), 2nd, Ermine two chevrons azure (Bagot), 3rd, Argent two chevrons azure (Bagot)
Crest, mantling and motto: As 1.   The hatchment bears the initials L.C. and the date 1655
For Lewis Chadwick, who m. Mary, dau. and heir of Anthony Bagot, of Colton, and d. 1655.   (Sources, as 1.)

3. All black background

Qly, 1st and 4th, Chadwick, 2nd, Or on a chief per pale gules and azure three bezants (Kyrkeshagh), 3rd, Gules four lozenges engrailed in bend ermine (Heley)   in pretence: Qly, 1st and 4th, Chadwick, 2nd, Cawarden, 3rd, Malveysin
Crest and mantling: As 1.   Motto: Crede mihi   The hatchment bears the initials I.C. and the date 1668
For John Chadwick of Healey, Lancs, who m. Katharine, only dau. and heiress of Lewis Chadwick, and d. 1668.   (Sources, as 1.)

4. All black background

Qly, 1st and 4th, Chadwick, 2nd, Kirkeshagh, 3rd, Heley, impaling, Qly, 1st, Argent on a saltire azure within a bordure gules five water bougets or (Sacheverell), 2nd, Gules a duck argent (Snitterton), 3rd, Gules a pale lozengy argent (Statham), 4th, Argent a lion rampant sable crowned or charged on the shoulder with a crescent or (Morley)
Crest and mantling: As 1.   Motto: En bon foy   The hatchment bears the date 1697
For Charles Chadwick, who m. 1665, Anne, only dau. of Valence Sacheverell, of New Hall, and d. Feb. 1697.   (Sources, as 1.)

5. All black background
Qly of six, 1st and 5th, Chadwick, 2nd, Malveysin, 3rd, Cawarden, 4th,
Argent a chevron gules between three martlets sable (Bagot), 6th,
Sacheverell, impaling two coats per fess, in chief, Azure seven garbs,
four, two and one or (Dolman) and in base, Azure a chevron between
three lozenges argent (Illingworth)
Crest and mantling: As 1.   Motto: Virtute nulla possessio
major   The crest is flanked by the date 1756
For Charles Chadwick, who m. 1st, 1699, Dorothy, dau. of Sir Robert
Dolman, of Shaw House, Berks, and 2nd, 1714, Mary, dau. of Robert
Illingworth, and d. 24 Dec. 1756.   (Sources, as 1.)

6. All black background
Qly, 1st, Chadwick, 2nd, Malveysin, 3rd, Sacheverell, 4th,
Morley   In pretence: Qly, 1st, Argent on a bend engrailed sable
three fleurs-de-lys argent (Holt), 2nd, Argent three bulls passant sable
(   ), 3rd, Gules a fess between three shovellers argent (Herle), 4th,
Per pale argent and gules three towers counterchanged (Prideaux)
Crest: A talbot's head gules collared gules and azure pierced through
the neck with an arrow or   Mantling: As 1.   Mottoes: (above
crest) Juxta salopiam   (below shield) Stans cum rege   The
hatchment has the date 1800 and the initials I.C.
For John Chadwick, who m. Susannah, dau. of Robert Holt of
Sherrington, and d. 23 Nov. 1800.   (Sources, as 1.)

7. Sinister background black
Qly, 1st, Chadwick, 2nd, Malveysin, 3rd, Sacheverell, 4th,
Morley   In pretence: Qly, 1st and 4th, Argent on a chevron between
three fleurs-de-lys azure three escallops argent (Green), 2nd, Azure a
stag trippant argent between three bezants (Redshaw), 3rd, Argent on a
bend engrailed azure two trefoils or (Bolt)
Mantling: As 1.   Motto: Resurgam   Shield surmounted by a
cherub's head and winged skull below   The hatchment bears the
date 1804 and the initials F.C.
For Frances, dau. and heiress of Richard Green of Leventhorpe House,
Yorks, who m. Charles Chadwick, and d. 1804.   (Sources, as 1.)

8. All black background
Qly, 1st, Chadwick, 2nd, Cawarden, 3rd, Malveysin, 4th, Holt   In
pretence: Qly, 1st and 4th, Green, 2nd, Sable a stag or between three
bezants (Redshaw), 3rd, Argent on a bend engrailed sable two trefoils or
(Bolt)
Crest: A talbot's head gules   Mantling: As 1.   Motto:
Resurgam   Skull in base   The hatchment is dated 1829
For Charles Chadwick, widower of 7., who d. 1829.   (Sources, as 1.)

9. Dexter background black

Qly, 1st, Chadwick, 2nd, Malveysin, 3rd, Sacheverell, 4th, Green, impaling, Qly, 1st and 4th, Per chevron argent and gules a crescent argent (Chapman), 2nd, Gyronny of six ermine and azure a dolphin embowed counterchanged (   ), 3rd, Argent a chevron gules between three trefoils slipped sable (   )
Crests: (each with motto) 1. A lily argent stalked and leaved proper   Motto: In candore decus   2. A talbot's head gules collared argent with ribbons gules, the collar charged with three cronels gules, pierced through the neck with an arrow or   Motto: Juxta salopiam   Mantling: As 1.   Motto: (below shield) Stans cum rege   The hatchment has the initials H.M.C. at top and the date 1854 in base
For Hugo Malveysin Chadwick, who m. Eliza Catherine Chapman, and d. 1854.   (Sources, as 1.)

10. All black background

On a lozenge surmounted by a lover's knot and flanked by two palm branches
Arms: As 9.   The hatchment is dated 1868 in base
For Eliza Catherine Chadwick, widow of 9., who d. 1868.   (Sources, as 1.)

PATTINGHAM

1. All black background

On a lozenge   Per fess argent and gules in chief three roundels sable (Boycott), impaling, Sable three molets argent (Puleston)
For Jane, youngest dau. of John Puleston, who m. 1763, Thomas Boycott, of Boycott, and d. Oct. 1803.   (B.L.G. 7th ed.)

2. All black background

Gules on a chief argent three grenades fired proper (Boycott), impaling, Gules a chevron ermine between three cinquefoils or (Tarleton)
Crest: Issuant from a mural coronet an arm in armour embowed casting a grenade proper   Mantling: Gules and argent   Motto: Pro rege et religione   Cherub's head in base
For Thomas Boycott, who m. 1801, Jane, eldest dau. of Thomas Tarleton, of Bolesworth Castle, co. Chester, and d. 24 Apr. 1856.   (B.L.G. 7th ed.)

RUGELEY. Wolseley Hall

1. All black background

Argent a talbot passant gules langued sable in dexter chief the Badge of Ulster (Wolseley), impaling, Gules two bars between three pheons argent (   )
Crest: From a ducal coronet or a wolf's head gules langued sable   Mantling: Gules and argent   Motto: In coelo quies
Unidentified

2. Dexter background black
Wolseley, with Badge of Ulster in chief, impaling, Barry of eight sable
and or (Selby)
Crest: From a ducal coronet or a talbot's head proper langued
gules   Mantling: Gules and argent   Motto: Homo homini
vulpes
For Sir Charles Wolseley, 8th Bt., who m. 1834, Mary Anne, dau. of
Nicholas Selby of Acton House, Middlesex, and d. 1854.   (B.P.
1949 ed.)
(The Hall is now demolished and the present whereabouts of the
hatchments is unknown)

RUSHTON SPENCER

1. Dexter background black
Qly, 1st and 4th, Azure three pheons and a canton argent (Nicolls), 2nd
and 3rd, Argent a griffin segreant gules armed and langued azure
(Trafford)
No helm   Crest: A wolf's head erased sable langued gules collared
with a band of five ermine tails or   Mantling: Gules and
argent   In an oak frame
Probably for Edward Nicolls, of Swythamley Park, eldest son of
William Nicolls, of Colton Hall and Whitgreave, by Sarah, only dau.
and heiress of William Trafford, of Swythamley Park, who m. Ellen,
dau. of William Taylor, of Liverpool, and d. 21 Mar. 1806.   (John
Sleigh, *A History of the Ancient Parish of Leek in Staffordshire*, 1883; Par.
Regs.)

2. Dexter background black
Per pale argent and sable three chevrons engrailed between three brocks
statant all counterchanged, in centre chief the Badge of Ulster
(Brocklehurst)   In pretence: Per chevron gules gutty argent and or,
in chief three escallops or and in base a mount vert and issuant
therefrom a fir-tree proper (Dewhurst)
Crest: A brock sable holding in the mouth a slip of oak fructed proper in
front of a mount vert thereon two oak trees proper   Mantling: Sable
and argent   Motto: Veritas me dirigit   In an oak frame
For Sir Philip Lancaster Brocklehurst, Bt., of Swythamley Park, who m.
1884, Annie Lee (d. 8 Aug. 1951), dau. of Samuel Dewhurst, of
Southfield Hall, co. Chester, and d. 10 May 1904.   (B.P. 1970 ed.)

SANDON

1. Dexter background black
Azure three crescents or each charged with an ermine spot sable
(Ryder)   In pretence: Gules three lapwings or (Terrick)
Baron's coronet   Crest: From a mural coronet or a dragon's head
argent charged on the neck with an ermine spot sable   Motto:
Servata fides cineri   Supporters: Two griffins argent each charged

with an ermine spot sable, each gorged with a plain collar azure charged with three crescents or, and chained or
For Nathaniel, 1st Baron Harrowby, who m. 1762, Elizabeth, dau. and co-heir of Richard Terrick, D.D., Bishop of London, and d. 20 June 1803.   (B.P. 1949 ed.)

2. Sinister background black
Qly, 1st and 4th, Ryder, 2nd and 3rd, Terrick, impaling, Qly, 1st and 4th, Barry of eight argent and gules over all a cross flory sable (Gower), 2nd and 3rd, Azure three laurel leaves erect or (Leveson)
Countess's coronet   Motto: As 1.   Supporters: Dexter, as 1.   Sinister, A wolf proper collared and lined or
For Susan, dau. of Granville, 1st Marquess of Stafford, who m. 1795, Dudley, 1st Earl of Harrowby, and d. 26 May 1838.   (B.P. 1949 ed.)

3. All black background
Arms: As 2.
Earl's coronet   Mottoes: As 1. and Resurgam   Supporters: As 2.
For Dudley, 1st Earl of Harrowby, who d. 26 Dec. 1847.   (B.P. 1949 ed.)

4. Sinister background black
Qly, as 2., impaling, Or a fess chequy azure and argent within a double tressure flory counter-flory gules (Stuart)
Countess's coronet   Supporters: As 1.
For Frances, 4th dau. of John, 1st Marquess of Bute, who m. 1823, Dudley, 2nd Earl of Harrowby, and d. 29 Mar. 1859.   (B.P. 1949 ed.)

5. All black background
Two shields   Dexter, within the Garter, Qly, as 2.   Sinister, within an ornamental wreath, as dexter, impaling, Stuart
Earl's coronet   Crest, motto and supporters: As 1.
For Dudley, 2nd Earl of Harrowby, K.G., who d. 19 Nov. 1882.   (B.P. 1949 ed.)

6. Dexter background black
Ryder, impaling, Barry of ten argent and azure six escutcheons, three, two and one sable each charged with a lion rampant argent (Cecil)
Earl's coronet   Crest, motto and supporters: As 1.
For Dudley Francis Stuart, 3rd Earl of Harrowby, who m. 1861, Mary Frances, eldest dau. of Brownlow, 2nd Marquess of Exeter, and d.s.p. 26 Mar. 1900.   (B.P. 1949 ed.)

7. Dexter background black
Ryder, impaling, Qly, 1st and 4th, Argent on a bend sable three mascles
argent (Dent), 2nd and 3rd, Or a chevron engrailed gules between three
trefoils slipped vert (Williamson)
Earl's coronet   Crest, motto and supporters: As 1.
For Henry Dudley, 4th Earl of Harrowby, who m. 1859, Susan Juliana
Maria Hamilton, only dau. of John Villiers Dent, of Barton Court,
Hants, and d. 11 Dec. 1900.   (B.P. 1949 ed.)

SEIGHFORD
1. All black background
Argent a chevron azure between three partridges close proper (Eld),
impaling, Azure on a bend between two lions rampant or three fleurs-de-
lys argent (Mootham)
Crest: A falcon rising or   Mantling: Gules and argent   Motto:
In coelo quies
For Francis Eld, of Seighford Hall, who m. 1794, Mary, dau. of John
Mootham, and d. 6 Jan. 1855.   (B.L.G. 5th ed.)

2. All black background
Eld arms only
Crest: As 1.   No mantling, but gold decoration representing leaves
and flowers   Motto: Resurgam
Probably for Francis Eld, eldest son and heir of Francis Eld, d. 5 May
1760.   (B.L.G. 5th ed.; G.M.)

SHUGBOROUGH Hall
1. All black background
On a lozenge   Vert three lions rampant reguardant argent ducally
crowned or (   )
Motto: In coelo quies   Much cut down and reframed; only part of
'o' of coelo and top of 'q' and 'u' of quies visible
Unidentified
(This hatchment was recorded in 1953, but its present whereabouts is
unknown)

STATFOLD
1. Dexter background black
Sable a fess wavy between three wolves' heads erased or
(Wolferstan)   In pretence: Argent a chevron between three escallops
sable (Littleton)
Crest: A wolf passant or under a tree proper   Mantling: Gules and
argent   Motto: In coelo quies
For Stanford Wolferstan, who m. Sarah, youngest dau. of Sir Edward
Littleton, Bt., and d. 2 July 1772.   (B.L.G. 2nd ed.)

TAMWORTH Castle
1. Dexter background black
Qly of sixteen, 1st, Azure a chevron ermine between three escallops argent (Townshend), 2nd, Qly gules and argent in the first quarter a molet or, a crescent for difference (Vere), 3rd, Sable a lion statant or between three helmets argent (Compton), 4th, Paly of six or and azure a canton ermine (Shirley), 5th, Argent a fess and in a chief three annulets gules (Devereux), 6th, Vairy gules and or (Ferrers), 7th, Azure three garbs or (Chester), 8th, Or an eagle displayed sable (   ), 9th, Gules seven lozenges, three, three and one or (Quincy), 10th, Gules a cinquefoil azure (Leicester), 11th, Gules a pale or (Grandesmil), 12th, Or a lion rampant within a tressure flory counter-flory gules (   ), 13th, Argent a cross gules between four water bougets sable (Bourchier), 14th, Argent a lion rampant sable (   ), 15th, France quartering England a bordure argent (Plantagenet), 16th, Azure a bend argent cotised or between six lions rampant or (Bohun), impaling, Or a fess chequy argent and azure within a royal tressure gules (Stuart)
Marquess's coronet   Crest: A stag trippant or   Motto: Haec generi incrementa fides   Supporters: Dexter, A stag sable attired or   Sinister, A greyhound argent
For John, 4th Marquess Townshend, who m. Elizabeth Jane, dau. of Rear-Admiral Lord George Stuart, and d. 10 Sept. 1863.   (B.P. 1963 ed.)
(There is another hatchment for the 4th Marquess at East Raynham, Norfolk)

TRENTHAM
1. Dexter background black
Two shields   Dexter, within the Garter, Qly, 1st and 4th, Barry of eight argent and gules a cross patonce sable (Gower), 2nd, Azure three leaves or (Leveson), 3rd, Gules three molets a bordure or charged with a royal tressure gules (Sutherland)   Sinister, as dexter, impaling, Qly of six, 1st, Gules on a bend between six cross crosslets fitchy argent the augmentation of Flodden (Howard), 2nd, Gules three lions passant guardant or a label of three points argent (Brotherton), 3rd, Chequy or and azure (Warren), 4th, Gules a lion rampant argent (Mowbray), 5th, Gules three escallops argent (Dacre), 6th, Barry of six argent and azure three chaplets gules (Greystock)
Duke's coronet   Crests: Dexter, A goat's head erased ermine   Centre, A wolf passant argent collared and lined or   Sinister, A wild cat sejant proper   No mantling   Motto: Frangas non flecte   Supporters: Dexter, A wolf argent collared and lined or   Sinister, A savage wreathed around the waist with leaves, the dexter hand holding a club over his shoulder, the sinister supporting an antique shield charged with the arms of Sutherland
For George, 2nd Duke of Sutherland, who m. Harriet Elizabeth Georgiana, dau. of George, 6th Earl of Carlisle, and d. 22 Feb. 1861.   (B.P. 1963 ed.)

TRYSULL
1. All black background
Vert a chevron between three molets or, on a canton argent a lozenge
azure (Pudsey)
Crest: A cat-a-mountain passant guardant proper charged on the
shoulder with a lozenge or   Mantling: Gules and
argent   Motto: Fortuna favente
For either Thomas Peach Aston, of Seisdon Hall, who assumed name
and arms of Pudsey in 1807, and d. unm. Mar. 1846, or his brother,
John Aston, of Seisdon Hall, who assumed name and arms of Pudsey in
1846, and d. unm. 17 Mar. 1861.   (B.L.G. 1886 ed.)

UTTOXETER
1. Dexter background black
Qly, 1st and 4th, Azure on a chevron or between three fleurs-de-lys
argent three molets of six points gules (Sheppard), 2nd and 3rd, Argent
a bend between three roundels sable (Cotton), over all the Badge of
Ulster, impaling, Sable ermined argent on a cross quarter-pierced argent
four millrinds sable (Turner)
Crests: Dexter, A lamb passant argent   Sinister, A falcon wings
elevated and inverted or   Mantling: Sable and argent   Motto:
Resurgam
For Sir Thomas Cotton-Sheppard, 2nd Bt., who m. Mary Anne, dau. of
the Rev. George Turnor of Wragby, and d. 5 Apr. 1848.   (B.P. 1849
ed.)

WALSALL Public Library
1. Dexter background black
Argent on a fess gules cotised azure between three Catherine wheels
sable three lambs passant argent, the Badge of Ulster (Scott), impaling,
Or ermined sable a lion rampant sable langued gules, on a canton sable
a garb or (Gisborne)
Crest: A beacon fired proper   Mantling: Gules and
argent   Motto: Resurgam
For Sir Edward Dolman Scott, 2nd Bt., who m. 2nd, 1848, Lydia, dau.
of the Rev. Thomas Gisborne, of Yoxall Lodge, and d. 27 Dec.
1851.   (B.P. 1963 ed.)
(This hatchment was recorded in 1953, but its present whereabouts is
unknown)

WESTON-UNDER-LIZARD
1. Sinister backgound black
Qly of six, 1st, Sable ten roundels four, three, two and one argent, on a
chief argent a lion passant sable (Bridgeman), 2nd, Argent a lion
rampant sable (Kynaston), 3rd, Azure three lions rampant or, on a chief
argent three cross crosslets sable (Matthews), 4th, Argent a chevron or
between three leopards' faces sable (Newport), 5th, Argent three bends
wavy azure (Wilbraham), 6th as 1st, in fess point the Badge of Ulster,

impaling, Qly, 1st and 4th, Qly per fess indented argent and sable in
the first and fourth quarters a buglehorn sable stringed or (Forrester),
2nd and 3rd, Azure a fess nebuly argent between three crescents ermine
(Weld)
Countess's coronet   Motto: Nec temere nec timide   Supporters:
Two leopards proper semy of roundels sable
For Selina, dau. of Cecil, 1st Baron Forester, who m. Orlando, 3rd Earl
of Bradford, and d. 25 Nov. 1894.   (B.P. 1963 ed.)

WHITMORE
1. All black background
Argent two bars gules (Mainwaring), impaling, Qly, 1st and 4th, Argent
a lion rampant gules (Macduff), 2nd and 3rd, Azure a fess dancetty
ermine between in chief a stag's head cabossed and in base two escallops
or (Duff)
Crest: From a ducal coronet or an ass's head couped proper haltered
argent   Motto: Devant si je puis
For Rear-Admiral Rowland Mainwaring, who m. 1st, 1810, Sophia
Henrietta (d. 11 Oct. 1824), only child of Major William Duff, and 2nd,
1826, Mary Anne (d. 8 Jan. 1835), 2nd dau. of John Clark, of Preshute,
Wilts, and 3rd, 1836, Laura Maria Walburga Julia (d. 17 Mar. 1891),
only child of Florian Chevillard, and d. 11 Mar. 1862.   (B.L.G.
1937 ed.)

2. All black background
On an asymmetrical lozenge surrounded by ornamental scrollwork
Mainwaring arms only
For Sarah, eldest dau. of William Mainwaring (d. 1812), who d. unm.
31 Mar. 1837, aged 63.   (B.L.G. 1937 ed.)

WHITMORE Hall
1. All black backgound
Argent two bars gules (Mainwaring), impaling, Argent on a bend sable
three chessrooks argent (Bunbury)
Crest: From a ducal coronet or an ass's head haltered
proper   Mantling: Sable and argent   Motto: Devant si je
puis   Winged skull in base   On wood panel
For Edward Mainwaring, of Whitmore, who m. 1735, Sarah (d. 29 Nov.
1798), dau. and co-heir of William Bunbury, and d. 15 Apr.
1795.   (B.L.G. 18th ed.)

2. All black background
Mainwaring, impaling, Qly argent and gules four crosses formy
counterchanged (Chetwode)
Crest: As 1.   Mantling: Gules and argent   Motto: As
1.   Winged skull in base

For Edward Mainwaring, of Whitmore, who m. Anne (d. 7 Feb. 1816), eldest dau. of Sir Philip Touchet Chetwode, 2nd Bt., and d. Dec. 1825.   (B.L.G. 18th ed.)

3. All black background
Mainwaring arms only
Crest, mantling and motto: As 2.   Winged skull in base
Either for Charles Henry Mainwaring, d. unm. 25 Feb. 1889, or his brother, Frederick Rowland Mainwaring, d. unm. 2 May 1891.   (B.L.G. 18th ed.)

SELECT BIBLIOGRAPHY

P. G. Summers, *How to read a Coat of Arms* (National Council of Social Service, 1967), 17-20.

P. G. Summers, *The Genealogists' Magazine*, vol. 12, No. 13 (1958), 443-446.

T. D. S. Bayley and F. W. Steer, 'Painted Heraldic Panels', in *Antiquaries Journal*, vol. 35 (1955), 68-87.

L. B. Ellis, 'Royal Hatchments in City Churches', in *London and Middlesex Arch. Soc. Transactions* (New Series, vol. 10, 1948), 24-30 (contains extracts from a herald-painter's work-book relating to hatchments and 18th-century funerals).

C. A. Markham, 'Hatchments', in *Northampton & Oakham Architectural Soc. Proceedings*, vol. 20, Pt. 2 (1912), 673-687.

INDEX